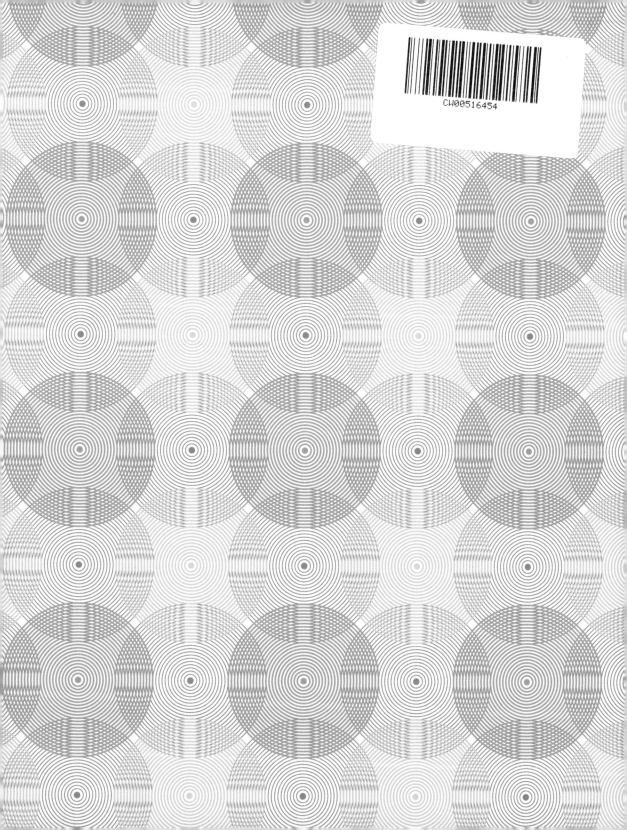

The

JOY

of

MINDFUL

SEX

The

JOY

of

MINDFUL

SEX

Be in the moment
& enrich
your lovemaking

CLAUDIA BLAKE

Leaping Hare Press

First published in the UK in 2010 by
Leaping Hare Press
210 High Street, Lewes
East Sussex BN7 2NS, UK
www.leapingharepress.co.uk

British Library Cataloguing-in-Publication Data
A catalogue record for this book is available from
the British Library

ISBN: 978-1-907332-36-4

This book was conceived, designed, and produced by
Leaping Hare Press

Creative Director Peter Bridgewater
Publisher Debbie Thorpe
Art Director Wayne Blades
Senior Editor Polita Anderson
Designer Bernard Higton

All images © Getty Images

Printed in Hong Kong
Colour Origination by Ivy Press Reprographics

10 9 8 7 6 5 4 3 2 1

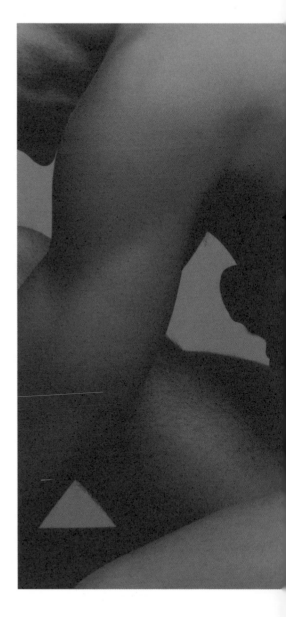

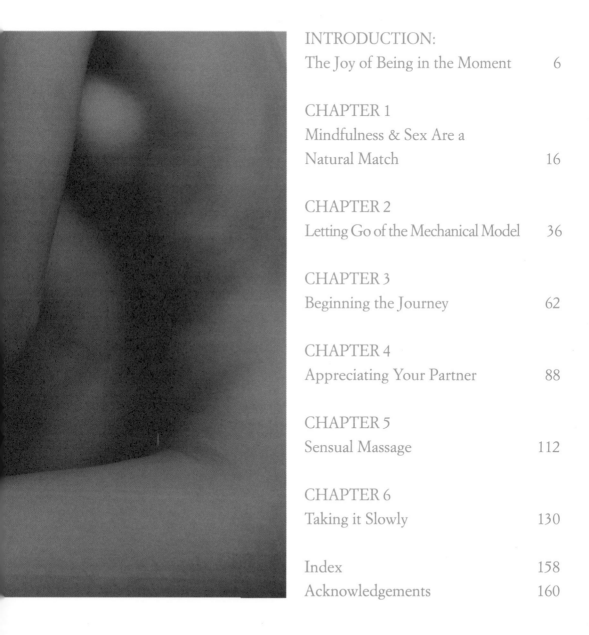

Contents

Sex has always been and will always be amongst the deepest and most powerful of human drives. Many of us think about it constantly, yearning to be taken to a realm of perfect pleasure, for union with a beloved or for a time to be our wild, natural selves. We dream about a moment of delight that will let us transcend the daily grind and experience a more joyous consciousness.

Introduction: The Joy of Being in the Moment

What Holds Us Back?

We might think about sex a lot – but we also question ourselves: 'Am I sexy enough? Am I good in bed? Why can't we connect better?' At the back of our minds is often the fear that there's a 'right way' to do it, that others may be in on sexual secrets we lack. Most of us, too, long to bask in sexual admiration, to feel gorgeous and splendid – yet cling to the sad conviction that we are not that attractive. If we were thinner, we tell ourselves, if we were better endowed, if we were darker or fairer or bigger or smaller – maybe sex would be the blissfulness found merely in our dreams.

Within these two ideas – that there is a state of perfect sex we're not attaining, and that we're probably not attaining it because there's something wrong with us – lie all the sexual unhappiness we'll ever need.

Most of us already know this. We aren't stupid. We realise that self-criticism and perfectionism leads to discontent, and that blaming ourselves hurts our confidence more than it motivates us. We also know that these thoughts tend to make us more self-conscious and not as free and fun – in short, less sexy. It's easy to know these things, but it's another matter to do something about them.

Moving Away From the Familiar

We talk about 'changing our minds' as if our minds were coats that we could shrug off and renew without much effort. Certainly we can change conscious opinions, but sexual discontent isn't an opinion. It's a deep-rooted emotional habit, one that we feel and experience far more than we consciously cultivate. Indeed, if cultivating it were a conscious choice, we wouldn't choose to feel anything so distressing. As long as we're in that habit, the best sexual experience in the world can be only a temporary break; soon we're back with our original anxieties and sorrows, because these are the paths our minds are used to treading.

As long, in fact, as we let our minds wander down their familiar paths, we will be unable to shed our hesitations, our doubts and our discontents, precisely because they're familiar.

Imagine you are following your usual route one day, but you are then intending to turn off at the crossroads and visit a beautiful park. If you aren't paying attention to where you're going, what happens? Autopilot takes over – at the crossroads you miss your turning and keep heading the usual way. It's only when you 'come to', when you start paying attention to your surroundings, that you think, 'This isn't right. I'm stuck on a dull, cluttered street when I wanted to be surrounded by green trees and banks of flowers. How did I get here?'

The answer is simple: you needed to be mindful, aware of what is around you. Don't be discouraged. Finding yourself on the same dull street doesn't mean the park doesn't exist, nor that it has a guard at the gates set there to keep people like you out, nor that you can't find it if you try again. You need to find a different way of walking.

Finding That New Path

Sexual happiness is within our grasp.
It always has been. But to rejoice
in sex we have to be capable of
rejoicing – and to rejoice, we have to
be at peace with ourselves. This is
where mindfulness practice comes in.
As we journey through the process,
we need to let go of preconceptions
and expectations. What we expect
for the future only distracts us from
the now. Take a deep, calming breath
and let yourself settle. The road ahead
is unpredictable, but when we are free
within ourselves nothing along the way
will harm us.

To Keep in Mind

This book isn't an inflexible guide. All of us differ in our sexual tastes and longings; a one-size-fits-all guide ends up fitting nobody. Rather than laying out a rigid sequence of steps to follow, the book will guide you into finding and enjoying your own way. Mindfulness rather than technique is the key.

When we talk of sexual mindfulness and meditation, many will picture something unattainable: elaborate positions, years of training to achieve hour-long orgasms and uncomfortable-looking contortions that may sound like fun but that look dauntingly difficult to accomplish. Whilst there's no reason not to look deeper into such things if your interest lies that way, they are not what this book is about. Rather than changing your sexual activities as such, with simple mindfulness you can experience a world of newness and pleasure without having to push your body to extremes.

A Note on Sexual Orientation

There are many sexual identities: heterosexual, gay, bisexual, transsexual. Mindfulness is exclusive to none of them. However the majority of people are straight, so this book will sometimes assume a couple is heterosexual simply because this is statistically the likeliest. It is in the nature of mindfulness to know and accept our real selves. No one sexuality is the 'right' one. Suiting the practices to our own sexuality will always be a part of the journey.

Mindfulness Spans All Cultures

Neither is this book about Eastern philosophies and religions. Mindfulness is not the province of any one culture but is the natural capability of all humanity. This book is written for a Western audience in terms familiar to the average Westerner in the process of discovering just how extraordinary the 'average' human being can be.

To be mindful we must begin where we are with who we are: the minute we conclude that another culture is wiser than our own, we are looking outside ourselves for the wisdom we can better find within.

Safety First

Being in the moment should never mean resigning responsibility for your future safety. Our bodies are precious, and we must never be negligent about keeping them out of danger.

Although there is greater awareness of sexual diseases nowadays, many of us would rather push the idea out of our minds. We struggle, too, with the idea that great sex means being 'swept away', too overwhelmed to think of anything else – including the necessary question, 'Where are the condoms?'

Yet both of these ideas go against mindfulness. The first is simply denial, and denial is based on the fear that we can't handle our own feelings if we face facts. These fears are simply your body trying to protect itself, and are not a sign that you are unsexy or overly worried. Instead, feel what you feel, and respect the risks but don't allow them to dominate your thoughts.

Safety and Enjoyment

The second pernicious idea is that if we're truly 'in the moment', we won't be thinking of safety measures. Yet mindfulness, as we'll discover, is not about thinking the right things. Any thought or feeling can be experienced with mindfulness. In this kind of love-making a pause for precautions is not an interruption of the flow; it is simply one of many ripples that merge together to make up the whole. A gesture of respect for the health of your body and your lover's can be made with just as much mindfulness and tenderness as any other part of the experience.

Make it the Perfect Fit

Here's a simple example of how
mindfulness and safe sex work together.
Many men have bad associations with
condoms, and a reason for this is that
many haven't found condoms that fit.
A 2008 study by the University of
Indiana shows that 18 per cent of
European men found condoms were
too short and 7 per cent found them
too long, whilst 21 per cent found
the fit of condoms too tight and
10 per cent found them too loose.[1]

Given these problems, it's hardly
surprising that men aren't always
eager to reach for the protection;
after all no one likes to dance in
ill-fitting shoes! A manufacturer
is being unmindful of reality if it
assumes that one size of condom
will fit every man; likewise a man
is unmindful if he grabs the nearest
box on the shelf. Fortunately
nowadays there is a good variety
of different sizes and shapes. With
an attentive search, comfortable
protection is yours for the taking.

Safety and Massage

If you're unsure of your partner's
history and you're practising genital
massage, which we'll be discussing in
later chapters, it's a good idea to wear
rubber gloves. Massage is a lower-risk
activity than penetrative sex, but it's
not risk-free. Surgical gloves are light
and inexpensive, and can be bought
in bulk through medical suppliers or
online. Similarly if you want to try anal
massage or penetration, it's a good
idea to wear gloves, or a condom over
your finger. Even if you are sure of
your partner's history, the anus and
anal passage contain plenty of bacteria
that can get under fingernails, so it's
best to preserve hygiene.

Also note that when it comes to
massage, the golden rule is that oil and

latex don't mix. If you're planning
on some genital contact alongside
your massage, it's wise to use talcum
powder rather than oil – which will
weaken the condom and increase
the chances of leaks or splitting –
to make your hands glide.

Oil isn't overly good to introduce
into the vagina either, so if you're
practising a genital massage, it's best
to choose a water-based lubricant. The
cheaper of these tend to dry out fairly
fast, but silicone-based ones last longer.

None of this needs be a squeamish
business. The human body is a
complex and delicate creation,
and nothing about it is distasteful
unless we distract ourselves with
unrealistic notions of a sanitized,
'perfect' thing that has nothing
to do with the vital and compelling
drama of real flesh. Protecting
ourselves is simply one step in the
dance, no less graceful than any other.

A Word About Terminology

There are very few words in the English language that describe sex well, and there is a particular dearth of good words for the sexual organs. There are plenty of euphemisms, vulgar expressions and slang terms but, on the whole, talking about sex isn't something that many of us find easy. We can joke about it, we can curse, we can blush and stammer, but it's a symptom of our discomfort with all things sexual that we really lack any words that are simply neutral. Say the word 'arm', and nobody bats an eyelid. But any synonym for the genitals tends to leap off the page, jarring with the other words in the sentence.

This is unfortunate. Your lover's genitals are an essential part of him or her, harmoniously integrated into the body, but it's very difficult to express the elegant wholeness of the human body in words.

So What Words to Use?

We have to work with what we have. This book will therefore use the basic medical terms – penis, labia, clitoris and so forth. These are not considered very pretty words and can often feel clinical. However, some of the massages described will go into detail, and using softer sounding Sanskrit words for the genitals such as '*yoni*' or '*lingam*' would lack precision; it would be like trying to describe how to massage a lover's lips, nose, eyebrows and forehead whilst using only the word 'face'.

The fact that we find these words cold has a lot to do with the fact that we usually only hear them from doctors. When talking with friends and family, we're happy to mention arms and legs, but discussion of the more intimate parts is usually not an option, so we never have the chance to become used to the correct terminology. We often

fall back on joking terms to cover
our discomfort, and only hear the
serious words when we need to
discuss a health issue. If the word
'foot' was unmentionable in polite
society, no doubt it would also
sound clinical when we heard it.

If the words feel uncomfortable
to you, try this: take a moment to
sit comfortably, close your eyes
and repeat the difficult word in
your head. Say it over and over,
imagining it recited by a soft, gentle
voice. Create a safe space for yourself,
and make friends with the word.

Of course the fact that this book
uses these particular words doesn't
mean that you must. Discussing how
you feel about language is a wonderful
way to confront and move past your
initial embarrassment with your lover,
and if you feel happy doing so, you
can choose expressions of your own,
finding the words that suit you best.

Moving Beyond Words
More than that, though, you don't
need to name every part that you
touch when you and your partner
are making love. Once you're in
motion you aren't talking with your
voice, you're talking with your body.
Your hands, your mouth and your
skin are wiser than your vocabulary,
and know full well that every part
of your lover is an element of the
greater whole, special but united.
Language can't really express this,
but our bodies understand it.

15

Taught first by the Buddha over two-and-a-half millennia ago, today the practice of mindfulness is studied in disciplines as various as yoga, stress reduction, chronic pain management and substance abuse therapy. The reason for this thriving divergence is easy: it works.

So what is it? Simply, it is a state of being aware. When we are aware, or mindful, we are in the present moment. How easy that sounds! But human beings are distractible creatures. Worries about the future, thoughts of the past, critical value judgements, plans and aspirations – all of them scurry through our consciousness, coming between our selves and the world, and between our brains and our spirits.

1. *Mindfulness & Sex Are a Natural Match*

Mindfulness lets us ride out these distractions, to let go of stray thoughts and to just be, feel and let ourselves exist as we are: not to be as we should be, not to be as we wish we were, but to be here, now – present, vital and real.

And What Is More Vital to Us than Sex?

Sex is the generative act through which life springs anew. Sex is the intimacy of body to body, the close embrace that bonds us to those we care for most. Sex is the pleasure we give to others and to ourselves: the ultimate delight of flesh and feelings together. The more deeply we can experience it, the more loving, refreshing and delicious it becomes.

Life can separate us from our bodies: with mindfulness, we can come home to them again.

Becoming Mindful

Stop a minute. Take a moment to consider your surroundings. How does this book feel in your hands? What can you smell, hear, taste? Can you feel the movement of your body as you breathe? Wait for a few seconds before you proceed to the next paragraph and just perceive everything around you.

The experience you've just had was a moment of mindfulness. It's as simple and as profound as that.

Going Through the Motions

The human mind tends to switch to autopilot. Being the extraordinary creation it is, the brain can steer the body through an extremely complex series of manoeuvres without really perceiving them, especially if those manoeuvres are familiar. It's something of a miracle of evolution: as you read these words hundreds of thousands of people are driving to work, washing the dishes, performing a multitude of advanced tasks – without even paying attention. The experience is familiar to all of us. How often have you come to the end of a journey knowing you must have made all the usual turns but with no memory of making them? Perhaps you were daydreaming, or perhaps your mind was on past events or on plans for the future. But wherever you were, it wasn't here and now.

Tuning In to the Present

In new situations we're far less able to do this. If you want to follow a route you've never followed before, you need to pay attention if you don't want to get lost. When circumstances demand it, we're right there in the present moment. Events become vivid and absorbing.

But here's the truth: every moment is new. Every instant that passes is different, utterly itself, absolutely unique and perfect in its own way. We just need to open our eyes to see.

Imagine this: you have a letter to mail, so you head to a post box. On your way there you're running on autopilot. Not much is passing through your mind: your feet follow their usual route without any prompting, and you get to the post box easily enough. But as you put the letter in the post box, feeling the cold metal against your hand and hearing the soft click of paper landing on paper, you realize you simply can't remember walking there.

On the way home you decide to pay more attention. You feel the impact of the pavement under your feet. The clouds flicker over the sun, taking the light from warm and dazzling to cool and clear. A sparrow rustles in the shrub to your left. Your arms are cosy and warm in their sleeves. There is a world of interest and delight all around you – and if you'd gone home as absentmindedly as you'd left, you would have missed it!

The World on Our Doorstep

When we take the time to focus the world becomes extraordinary. The pavement under your feet is concrete – a liquid stone shaped by human design. The clouds above your head are flying water, passing before the sun, a ball of roaring fire that nourishes all the life on Earth. The sparrow is as vitally alive as you or I, flitting fast through its own existence. Your arms are you, a mass of nerves and fibres that respond precisely to every stimulus and every command. Whichever way you turn your head, there are wonders.

Mindfulness is a practice, one that brings great spiritual benefits, but it's far from dry or moralistic. In this beautiful world a moment of mindfulness is a treat. Alert and awake, we open ourselves to the marvel that is our ordinary and everyday reality.

Non-judgement

When we are mindful we are present in all our senses, open to all our perceptions. And this includes the perception of something we often forget to categorize – our thoughts.

If we're drifting in a haze, our thoughts probably aren't doing very much. But human beings have big, active brains – and one of the favourite tricks our thoughts can pull off is to pass a judgement. No sooner does a sensation enter the mind, then 'click', it triggers a reaction, and that reaction is frequently an assessment of some kind.

This is Natural
Human beings are animals and have evolved in a world where making judgements and decisions was once crucial to survival. For example, a sweet berry was found to be better to eat than a bitter poisonous one; a tree with leaves provided better shelter from the rain than a bare one; a person in the tribe was safer company than a stranger. All were judgement calls we needed to make to deal with threats.

Unfortunately, however, our big brains have the habit of throwing judgements around at every single stimulus, even when there's no need, particularly in the modern world. For example, 'The sound of a branch tapping on a window is better than the sound of that passing car' is not a survival decision when we're safe inside our own houses.

Stay in the Direct Experience
When we are present and calm in the world, we do not need to assess threats. We are here, in the moment and we are safe. What these judgements do is move us from direct experience to interpretation. We withdraw from hearing or feeling and enter into a conversation with ourselves about what we've just heard or felt –

and while we're talking to ourselves, we drown out the rest of the world. No longer alert and open we move from perception to compulsion. It becomes not 'I hear this', but 'I want to hear this', ... and as much in the world tends to be beyond our own control, this immediately courts frustration.

These judgements also separate us from the world. Instead of knowing ourselves to be a moving part of the living moment, we step back, weigh up and comment as if we were separate from reality, observing a show rather than participating in a dance. It is natural for us to form views on our experiences, so this may sound like bad news. How can we not have opinions? In fact the solution is more simple and graceful than one would think.

Non-judgement is far easier to understand in practice than in explanation, so let's begin with a simple meditation.

Breathing With Mindfulness

Sit yourself down comfortably. The position you choose for meditation is a matter of personal choice. Eastern religions favour the lotus position – legs crossed, feet folded up – and if this position is comfortable for you, by all means assume it as it's both stable and revered in many traditions. However, many Westerners find this a painful if not impossible position to get into, and there's no need to force yourself.

Alternative Positions
Try sitting cross-legged on a cushion, or fold several firm cushions together and kneel astride them, taking care the floor isn't too hard for your knees. Taking a poised position on a chair is fine too; you can meditate sitting on a bus seat if the spirit moves you. The main point of a meditation posture is that it should be sustainable without becoming so uncomfortable that it discourages you: follow the promptings

of your body to find what works best for you. Let your head drift upwards as if pulled by a string, your spine settling into position beneath: a comfortable posture will open your chest and let you remain in your stance without straining yourself. Lay your hands with palms up, close your eyes and begin.

Focus Attention on the Breath
Begin by noticing the exhalation. As the air sighs out of your lungs, feel how it affects your body. Does your stomach rise and fall? Does your chest lift? Can you feel the breath on your face as it leaves your body?

Continue doing this until you feel relaxed: as your body lets out its breath it should settle. Then move your attention to your inhalation. Is the air cool or warm in your throat? How does your body expand inside your clothes? Can you hear the sound of your breath as it draws in? Continue focusing on this, letting it fill your body with calm energy.

When you are ready, balance your attention so you are equally mindful of the in and the out breath. Don't try to guide it. Just let your body nourish itself with air in whatever rhythm feels natural to you, letting your attention ride on the sounds and sensations.

Finally move your mindfulness up your body to the first place the breath touches it. Do you feel the rush of air through your nostrils? Does it flow over your lips and tongue? Let your attention be absorbed as the life-giving air enters you, relaxing your mind to experience it completely.

All the time you're doing this be gently mindful of your surroundings. The feel of the floor beneath you, the noises of the world, all of these are part of the greater reality, as you are. Let them pass through you.

How Long Should You Do This?

As a beginner don't feel you have to spend hours – ten or fifteen minutes is a good starting time. Breathing meditations are one of the great foundations of mindfulness practice. When you are more experienced in them you can expand this meditation to as long as you choose.

As you focus on your breathing, you'll notice something almost inevitably happening – your mind will bring up observations. Remember this lesson and you will have mastered one of the key notes of mindfulness – you don't need to act on these thoughts.

On the most basic level there are concrete distractions. Unless you have a sealed bunker in your house, the chances are that there will be some background noise. That's fine: in fact, acknowledging the noise is an essential part of mindfulness meditation. The noise in itself won't distract you if you don't say to yourself, 'I'll never be able to concentrate with that lorry reversing in the street'. It isn't the lorry that's distracting you, it's the thought. Let the lorry get on with its business and you carry on with yours. Its noise is just one of the many things in your environment that your mindfulness is observing.

Let Thoughts Pass

Thoughts are the truly distracting thing, and they can pop up on a more abstract plane as well. If you find yourself thinking, 'Hey, this is great!' let yourself think that thought, let it pass away and carry on. If you find yourself thinking, 'I feel really stupid doing this', let yourself think that thought, let it pass away and carry on. If you find yourself thinking, 'I wonder if I've locked the door?' or 'I think I should have chosen a different sitting position', or 'What

does any of this have to do with sex?' let yourself think those thoughts, let them pass away and carry on.

The purpose of a meditation is not to control your thoughts. It is to not control your thoughts. The fact that you're having these thoughts doesn't mean the mindfulness experience isn't working: concentration is less like a crystal vase and more like a beloved puppy you're trying to keep in one place. It may wander off but if you quietly pick it up and bring it back, it'll stay there for a while longer. Your conscious thoughts are not your enemy as long as you don't see them as such. Like leaves floating by on a stream, they will bob along and move past us if we don't grab hold of them. The old saying, 'Don't just do something, stand there!' contains a profound lesson. It's easy to jump up and act on every passing thought – but sometimes what we need is to be still.

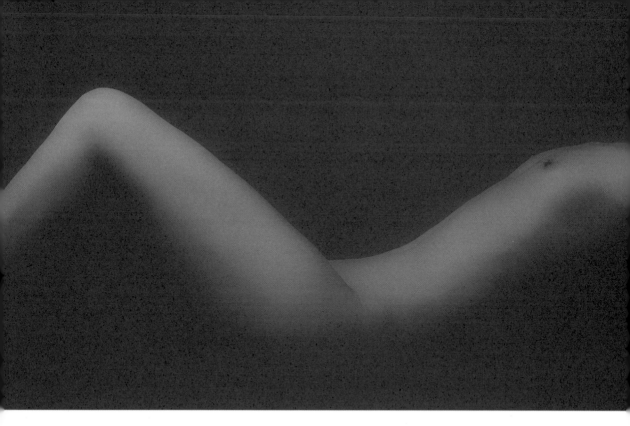

Simply Remain Present

Similarly meditation can bring up emotions. Sitting still and doing nothing can be an unnerving experience to a mind used to constant motion. As you sit you may find yourself feeling fear or tension. Perhaps the practice will make you angry. It puts demands on your patience and you don't feel like being patient just because some book told you to. Maybe you're excited or hopeful, maybe you're even full of joy. The purpose of mindfulness is not to produce or deny any of these emotions but to let them rise. Feel them while they are there, and when they begin to pass away let them go. If thoughts and feelings are the leaves on the stream, you are the sand below: everything flows over and around, but you remain present. Just sit and breathe. For a mindful moment let it be enough.

Congratulations. You've performed your first mindfulness meditation. Take a moment to assess how it affected you. And then let it go.

Every meditation will be slightly different – sometimes very different – from every other. As we continue with our practice of mindfulness and sexuality, it's important to try not to burden ourselves with expectations. If we expect mindfulness practice to work a magic spell that will make our every sexual encounter or meditation a mind-blowing revelation, we'll become quickly disappointed and discouraged. Similarly if we expect it to do no good at all, we're making a self-fulfilling prophecy; we're working on a state of mind, and it will be responsive to predictions of failure.

Try to Remain Non-judgemental
Handling our expectations of mindfulness practice should be as simple and non-judgemental as handling our thoughts as we meditate. 'This is going to be great!' or 'I bet this will be a waste of time' are, after all,

thoughts. They will pass through our minds – more leaves on the stream – but we must never mistake them for more than what they are: passing moments, expressions of our feelings at this precise moment. Yesterday you may have felt cynical and resistant; today you may feel inspired and excited. Who knows how you'll feel tomorrow? Our concern is with being in the present moment. The future will become its own present moment in due course and we'll experience it then.

As you continue to practise, the best line to take is simple open-minded, give-it-a-try willingness. The future is hard to predict, but deciding we know about it in advance won't help much; it just takes our minds off what we're doing now. Remember as you continue that no single meditation experience is the key to mindfulness. Every experience is itself and nothing more.

Mindfulness Practice: Letting Go of Judgement

Sit yourself down comfortably again. Arrange your body into a sustainable posture, lay your hands with palms upwards and focus on your breathing. Let the air come in and out of your body, let the world change around you, let your mind do whatever it chooses.

Chances are your mind will start putting in comments, and some of them will be judgements. When you find yourself making one – for example, 'This is working well' or 'I should have worn looser jeans for this' – note that you've made it. Don't condemn yourself. This is not an exercise in self-criticism. Your mind's tendency to form judgements is part of how it works: the trick is not to be judgement-free but to be unshaken by the judgements you make. So notice the judgement as you'd notice a sound outside, no more or less spontaneous, creating no more or less of a problem with your mindfulness.

Smile and Roll with It

Doing this you may find several other judgements occurring such as: 'Hmm, I noticed I made a judgement. That's good. Oh look, I just made another judgement, that's not so good. Oops, there goes another one. This is interesting, my mind's rattling away. Ah, "interesting", that's a judgement, isn't it?' And so on.

As your mind does this let your face assume a gentle smile. Smiling can have a powerful effect on our mood. A study in 2002 by scientist Robert Soussignan found that people rated amusing cartoons as funnier when they were smiling – even when the 'smile' was caused by being asked to hold a pen in their mouths![2] When your mouth smiles, your heart is warmed. So let yourself be rocked by your judgements and keep your face happy; they won't do you any harm as long as you don't cling to them.

Mindfulness in Action

Does this mean that the mindfulness way of life is sitting on a cushion? Far from it. When we are mindful we are alert and present in our minds – no matter what our minds or our bodies are doing. In the next chapter we'll begin to apply mindfulness to sexuality, but first it's necessary to understand how a mindful attitude can take place anywhere, under any circumstances.

The great Buddhist teacher Thich Naht Hanh has remarked that if you cannot meditate while you wash the dishes, you cannot meditate in silence.[3] This is the whole point of mindfulness: we are perceptive yet unshaken no matter what is happening to us or, indeed, what we are doing.

When we can understand that mindfulness is simply a state of mind, we will recognise that there is no such thing as a distraction. Just as the noisy lorry or the stray thought is just another experience to be recognised, so is the action of our hands washing a bowl or pulling up a weed; or our feet tapping on the dance floor or pounding the pavement to run for a bus. Just as the sounds around us, or our own thoughts, need not shake our mindful state, neither need our own activity.

Being In and Of the World
We are, after all, a part of the world. Distraction can limit our mindfulness to the haze of our own consciousness – or absentmindedness – but we remain, whether we notice it or not, an integrated fragment of the cosmic whole. If we want to be mindful of the world, this must always include mindfulness of ourselves: we are in and of the world. If the world need not be still for us to be mindful, neither need the part of the world that is us.

Nor do we need to cling to a specific meditation practice. Breathing is a long-established and particularly

helpful one, and we'll return to
variations of it later in the book, but
we can do anything meditatively. And
when we do mundane tasks transform
themselves into an experience of the
extraordinary. Sweeping the floor can
be a boring chore if we just want to
get it over with because our minds are
elsewhere, on a future state with the
floor already swept that doesn't exist.

But what does exist is the floor below,
with all its subtle variations of colour
and unique texture, the million
scattered shreds of dust that pile up and
tumble before the broom, the sound of
the brush's fibres swishing across the
floor, the feel of wood in our moving,
flexing hands. We can swing the broom
round and wish ourselves anywhere but
here, or we can dance with it into
reality, our minds a tranquil pool,
knowing that we cannot be anywhere
but here: here and now is where we are,
where we have always been.

Walking Meditation

Walking is an old and traditional meditation, and for our purposes an extremely valuable one. To experience your body in motion is the foundation of sensuality.

Decide on your route before you begin; making choices mid-walk involves judgement calls, and those are best kept out of meditation. Remember that you don't need to go the same way every time: in fact it's beneficial to choose different ways so you can experience for yourself the truth that it's equally possible to be mindful in a beautiful green park or on a busy city street.

Prepare your feet: make sure that you are wearing warm socks and a comfortable pair of shoes. Your feet will be carrying you through the journey, so it pays to treat them kindly. When you don your shoes breathe deeply and steadily – you are readying yourself.

Now Begin Your Walk

Feel the air as it smoothes over your skin, notice the bounce of your soles of your feet on the ground, the muscles of your legs. Let your breathing fall naturally into rhythm with your stride: four steps to the inhalation, four to the exhalation – or five, or six, depending on what feels most comfortable to you. Walk at a steady and easy pace: slow enough that you can experience your body working, but fast enough that you are walking like yourself.

You may find it useful to centre yourself by repeating a phrase silently in your head as you step. This need not necessarily be an esoteric mantra. If you are walking four steps to a breath for instance you could try, 'I walk in peace'. If five steps, you could try, 'This is my journey'. If six steps, perhaps, 'I am full of light'. Find a phrase that makes you feel right and walk with it.

Completing Your Journey

When you return to where you started, stop before you open the door, sit down or do whatever it will take to complete your journey. Stand still for a moment, taking in a deep breath and letting it go. Experience the sensation of your muscles cooling down after the gentle exercise, the different feel of the air on your face now you are still. Rest where you are for a few breaths, relaxing into your new state. Then go quietly back into your house, sit for a moment and carry on with your day.

If you have the solitude to finish with a sitting breathing meditation, this can be a lovely way to cool down. However, most of us have office colleagues and families who may claim our attention as soon as we walk in the door. This is no bad thing. We are connected to our fellow human beings and thrive on living

with them – and indeed it's possible to be mindful of our own selves even while talking to others. Doing a shut-eyed breathing meditation in front of them, though, is not very friendly, so ready yourself for the change from meditation to company – a few breaths' pause at the door can be a particularly good adjustment.

A great practical advantage of the walking meditation is that it can be slotted into the busiest of days. We need not begin at home or take ourselves to a special location: as in life we can always begin from where we are and find everywhere special. A short walking meditation can be carried out as you go to purchase your lunchtime sandwich or head home from the commuter train and is just as precious and valuable as the most elegant stroll in the world.

This is your life: where you walk is where you are.

A Final Word Before We Move On

Peace isn't something we learn by rote. It's something we experience. We can't learn by thinking about it or by reading about it. This is the way we absorb facts, but facts are of the intellect – and, as has already been remarked, the intellect is a weak ally when it comes to deepening our sensual joy.

When it comes to feeling and understanding we learn by doing. A moment of knowing in our spirits and in our flesh has a far deeper impact on us, gives us far steadier ground to stand on, than an intangible thought. For this reason it's important to keep on with mindfulness meditations. Rather than a theory one can master and then move on, mindfulness is a state of mind we return to in order to refresh ourselves.

An Exercise That Keeps Us Vital

As you continue you may discover that the earliest meditations seemed to be easier or more potent than subsequent ones. The phenomenon of 'beginner's mind' has long been recognised in Buddhism; doing something for the first time, we are open to what it is and nothing more, but as we keep doing it our ability to perceive it becomes loaded down with preconceptions. If this starts to happen, don't let it discourage you. Some meditations will always be easier or more pleasant than others: life is a constant stream of change. The most important thing is to remain mindful: 'This isn't going as well as yesterday', after all, is a thought that one can experience and release just as much as any other distraction.

Never condemn yourself or feel like a failure if you find a meditation hard to concentrate on. Your experience is always valid. Stay mindful and respect your own experience, and you will be your own safe place.

Here in the West we believe in sexual liberation. Our belief is sincere, but our actions are sometimes confused. On the one hand we want to be able to enjoy genuine freedoms, tolerance of alternative sexualities and rights for women, as well as to have access to reliable contraception.

At the same time we struggle. From every billboard, impossible beauties lean down. In one corner virginity is stigmatized as hopelessly pathetic: in another promiscuity is chastised as degrading and sinful. Jokes abound about how sex ends after marriage, yet adultery is roundly condemned. It seems there's no way we can win.

2. *Letting Go of the Mechanical Model*

What all these contradictions express is a deep and intense anxiety about sex. We want it but at the same time we don't feel good enough. Perfection glimmers in the distance, forever out of reach – and in our bones we believe that unless we are perfect enough, we aren't worthy of sexual happiness.

Live in the Present

As a people we like to believe that the future may be better than the present. It is this belief that has led to the genuine victories, the spread of sexual rights and freedoms – but as we turn from the present to the future we deny ourselves the opportunity for bliss that lies before us, here and now. Whilst we may indeed strive for a brighter day when it comes to freedom, pleasure in our own beds is a private experience. If we locate it outside ourselves in some other, better self, we rob ourselves of what was ours to begin with

Perfectionism

'The perfect is the enemy of the good.'
—Voltaire [4]

It's everywhere in our culture. From fairy stories where the prince and princess live happily ever after to porn actors who've starved, bleached, waxed, injected and implanted their bodies to a state of caricature, the message is with us – sexual joy is for the perfect. The imperfect, when it comes to public discussion of sex, seem to be invisible. If you're an ordinary person – and everybody in the world is ordinary and miraculous at once – it's very hard not to feel sometimes as if ecstasy is not for someone like you. Our sense of ordinariness can overshadow our sense of miracle, leaving us feeling disheartened and ashamed of our bodies.

In a way it's easy to understand the connection. Few things overwhelm us like passion – that state of happy glow after a truly satisfying encounter is an experience like no other. In that moment we do indeed feel as if we have everything we need, as if nothing could be wrong and everything is perfect.

Does Perfection Equal Pleasure?
The mistake we make is to tell ourselves that to feel that way again we have to be ready, to make ourselves perfect to pave the way for perfect satisfaction. The simple truth is that every person in the world is able to feel pleasure: pleasure is not an exclusive club but a universal capacity. We can all feel blissful. Our standards are just a little mixed up.

It doesn't help of course that we're so surrounded by images of perfect beauty – or more generally of the perfect man or woman. Whether it's the sculpted body that magazines promise us or the high-flying career an alpha male is supposed to have, advertisements are a big part of our life. An attractive woman recommends a brand of soap. This is innocent enough on the face of it but the implication is always clear. Buy this soap and you will become like, or become attractive to, a woman like this. Art critic John Berger has remarked that such advertisements operate by inciting envy. They encourage the buyer to envy an image of their future self, magically improved by ownership of the product. Which is to say such images have an impact, stealing our self-esteem and offering to sell it back to us for the price of whatever they're selling.[5]

This effect can end up fracturing our sense of self. On the one hand there is our imperfect, current self: on the other the fantasy self we are supposed to become. This is a rather complicated figure, given how many solicitations and standards have been set around it, but definitely not what we are now.

Where Mindfulness Comes In
To believe in a fantasy self that is beautiful, lovable and sexy is to tell ourselves that we are, in ourselves, ugly, unlovable and sexless. Sexiness does not depend on some process of change, and it isn't something that other people confer on us. Sexiness is, simply, the rich and vibrant capacity to enjoy feeling pleasure and the warm and enthusiastic ability to enjoy giving it.

This is a capacity that resides in all of us. Sexuality is felt and experienced, not perceived or attained. Whatever our pleasure, whatever our tastes, we have it in us to be as sexy, as earthy and as glorious and radiant as we could possibly want. We just need to glow from the inside out, not to build from the outside in.

What Holds Us Back?

Think of a baby in a bath. His little feet kick up glittering splashes of water, his arms churn in delight. He gurgles and coos at the pure sensual pleasure of the warmth on his skin. Think of a sturdy toddler running across a field. Her feet pound firmly and with confidence on the ground, celebrating her newfound ability to walk. The mere sight of an open space calls her to challenge and celebrate her body, and she laughs as she runs.

Walk through any park and you will see the playground, its slides built for no other purpose than for children to enjoy the pull of gravity on their bodies, its climbing frames built so children can proudly display the strength of their muscles, its swings hung so children can fly up into the sky with the wind rushing, cold and whistling, into their faces. So strong is our innate capacity for sensual pleasure, even before we

understand what sexuality is, that entire areas of land – temples to the sheer delight of being in our bodies and in this world – are set aside for it. We are born in physical joy.

How Do We Lose It?

To put it in a more uplifting way why should we lose it? As we grow from babyhood to maturity we gain in height and strength, in knowledge and wisdom. Nowhere is it written that we should also have to grow in sorrow and apathy. Coming into adulthood is an experience of addition, not of reduction, an increase in all our capacities. If a baby can do it, so can we.

As we move from infancy we learn many wonderful lessons. Those lessons are simply mixed in with other, darker ones, lessons that tell us to curtail our pride in ourselves for fear of humiliation to compare ourselves with others and come up wanting.

No one intends for us to forget our capacity for physical pleasure, but too often we take to heart the injuries and slights that tell us our bodies are not ours for the celebrating.

But if We Learn, We Can Unlearn

It is in the nature of the living to rejoice in their sensations, from a lizard basking, splayed and tranquil, in the heat of the hot golden sun, to a cat licking its fur clean, eyes closed in bliss. Whilst we like to think of ourselves as set apart, above the animal kingdom, such a choice closes us off not only from our intimacy with the world and our sense of ourselves as a natural part of the greater whole, but it detaches us from our bodies. We are animals, and animals thrive on pleasure. Before we knew how to speak, we knew how to feel and to love what we felt.

We gloried in ourselves once. We can do it again.

Body Image

We know what we're supposed to look like. A woman in our culture is expected to be thin but not bony, full-chested but not full-thighed. She must turn away from delicious food and deny the pleasures of her stomach and tongue if she wants to avoid the terrible sin of fat, but if her breasts lack fat she must hitch them up with padded underwear or seek out a surgeon. She must bake her skin brown if she is fair – but not age from sunlight: she must keep her skin light if she is dark. If her hair is straight, she must

pump up its volume in fear of its being 'lank': if it's curly, she must smooth it out in fear of its being 'frizzy' or 'kinky'. Eternally youthful, a woman's body is expected to be her life's work – and she must never let time defeat her. She must do all this, and yet she must never be satisfied in her work, for from the Middle Ages to today few accusations level a woman faster than the sin of vanity.

Expectations for a Man

A man in our culture is expected to be tall, muscular, his stomach ridged as a turtle's, and his muscles the product of hours in the gym (but not to care about his appearance either: if vanity is sinful in a woman, it is effeminate in a man). The thinness that would be prized in a woman is seen as weedy and unimpressive, but he mustn't be fat either. The texture of his skin must be manly and adult, but if too much hair grows on his chest or back he may seek out the services of a beautician and yank it all out with wax – though he must keep this a secret if he doesn't want to be shamed by laughter. Above all he must be the possessor of a prize penis, unflagging in its ability to rise to the occasion (but never rising unbidden and embarrassing him), precisely timed in its orgasms (never too soon, never too late), big enough to satisfy sexual partners and impress friends.

We all know these standards are unfair and impossible. We have all been attracted to people who don't fit this mould. Yet when it comes to judging ourselves we look in the mirror through hostile eyes, giving ourselves the gaze of a lover – but a lover about to reject us. The perfect body overlays our vision, and all we can see is the places where our own body fails to match up.

First Cultivate Love for Yourself

Living with Western body images and retaining a healthy love of our bodies – our faithful, reliable, constant bodies – is nothing short of heroic. To expect ourselves to step entirely free of such troubles in a single bound is almost as unrealistic as the body ideals themselves. However, cultivating love for our physical selves is essential. Our bodies are the instruments on which we play our blissful tunes, and we cannot play an instrument we are not comfortable with.

We need to let go of the idea that we must lose weight, gain muscle, whiten our teeth, dye our hair or wax our bikini line before we can love ourselves. Love is not a prize – it is a skill. If we cannot love ourselves as we are now, we are denying ourselves for no reason. Begin by accepting that your body is what it is, and loving it in its living present moment.

Self-Affirmation Exercises

Mirror Exercise

Most of us carry too much discomfort about our bodies to start off this exercise bare-skinned, and there is no need to put yourself under strain, so you may want to begin by doing it clothed and then work up to doing it naked. Stand before a mirror. Look yourself in the eyes and using your name say: 'Self, I love you exactly the way you are.' Say it out loud. Say it clear. Say it kindly and sincerely, as if you were reassuring a beloved child.

This simple exercise is surprisingly difficult. If you find it hard, if you start to cry or struggle, don't be alarmed. There is nothing wrong with you. You are simply reclaiming your natural self-love. Be brave and keep doing it.

Make a commitment to doing this exercise every morning and every evening. It takes less than a minute to perform, but as you do it you will begin to see your own beauty.

Walking Exercise

Perform a short breathing meditation, encouraging yourself to feel comfortable in your body. When you are ready, go for a short walk somewhere with plenty of people.

As you pass them by begin by feeling the sensuous swing of your own body. Cultivate a little strut that makes you feel good: if you feel slightly silly at the same time, that's fine – laugh at yourself and keep going. Fun is good.

Take a look at everyone you see. Who do you find attractive? What's nice about them? How many people can you see the beauty in?

Are Any of Them Perfect?

Use your eyes to teach yourself the simple truth: imperfect people are delectable. Whatever a poster or magazine calls for, humans see beauty in the bodies of real human beings. And that includes you.

A Word About Working Out

As far as mindfulness appreciation of yourself is concerned, there is no need to change a thing about your body. Exercise gurus tend to encourage us to work out to become thinner, bulk up, tone and trim, and generally move towards a new and better self. Peace be with them, but when it comes to mindfulness of self-love, the only thing you need to improve is your attitude.

Being Active Can Help

Yet a certain amount of physical exercise can do wonders for your self-esteem – not because it makes you look better, but because it lifts your mood. Doctors are now finding for instance that patients suffering from depression who do a certain amount of exercise (twenty minutes, three times a week is the figure usually recommended) show a marked improvement in their symptoms, as much as a mild dose of clinically prescribed antidepressants.[6]

Getting your body up and moving is giving yourself the opportunity to feel it testing itself, working on a high and renewing its energy. It's also an opportunity to feel by experience the heartening fact that, even though they may puff and pant, our bodies do in fact obey us. We are capable of more than we think.

For those who have no interest in sports and were always picked last for teams at school, the positive news is that one doesn't have to be any good at exercise to get something from it. Anything that speeds up the pulse and brings out a sweat, from fast walking to vigorous housework, will do it.

Set Your Own Pace

Competitive games are a lot of fun for those who enjoy them, but there is no need to prove yourself against others; in fact school sports are generally a bad way to introduce people to exercise because the fastest and strongest generally set the pace, leaving the slower ones struggling to keep up beyond their natural speed. Many people who felt for instance that they couldn't run – because they could never get around the school track – are astonished to discover that if they just set the pace a little lower, they can run and run and run. When it comes to exercise, being mindful of your body's natural pace is crucial to enjoying yourself.

If exercise is new to you, set your goals low enough that they won't intimidate you: a little bit of exercise you do regularly is much better than a lot of exercise you can never face. Exercise performed as a form of self-mortification, a punishment for sins against the great Beauty god, is not to be countenanced, but gentle exercise as a way of giving your body a little boost, as you'd water a plant and turn it to the light, can make you feel much happier in your skin.

Guilt

'To the pure in heart, everything is pure.'
—Kaulavali Nirnyana Tantra [7]

We in the West are the inheritors of a tradition that saw mind and spirit as opposites, even as natural enemies. For a long time we considered the pleasures of the senses to be the enemies of the soul – it was the soul we were meant to be concentrating on. If the soul was good and the body was opposed to the soul, then the body and anything that pleased it must be bad. Our bodies, innocently acting as they were created to do, were meant to be denied for the good of our souls. All kinds of awful words were created for sexual pleasure. Some were applied across the genders: fornication, self-abuse, self-pollution, lechery. Others involved mainly women, for example, slut, temptress and whore.

The violence of these feelings towards the body can never have been good for the soul: the human mind does not thrive on hatred. But as far as our sexual enjoyment went they cut an effective swathe. How can we enjoy something with a clean heart when our consciences, misled by guilt, are telling us that we are doing something wrong? Although we long for physical satisfaction, we are on the whole creatures of principle: we do not like to feel that our actions are genuinely bad.

But caught between the belief that gratifying the senses is wrong and the clamour of our senses for gratification, something has to give. All too often it is our peace of mind. We may or may not be able to stop ourselves from acting on our desires, but when we feel that desire itself is wrong, we become divided against ourselves, striving for some ascetic state of freedom from our bodies. This creates such a longing to get out of ourselves that we are unable to perceive with mindful freedom who and where we are.

Desiring Purity is Not Wrong

Our bodies are pure: simple, animal and natural, they desire sex as innocently as they desire water to drink and air to breathe. 'Pure' means uncontaminated, a thing that is simply itself and nothing other. When we come to sex mindfully, experiencing it as sex – uncontaminated with machismo, manipulation, violence or a need to prove ourselves – with an alert participation in the acts of our own flesh, sex becomes purely sex, a clean, physical act.

There is nothing wrong with striving for sexual virtue either. In fact it's easiest to be at peace with ourselves when our sexual behaviour does not go against our consciences. However, freedom from sexual guilt does not mean freedom from sexual principles. Therefore you should undertake a commitment to examine your beliefs. Whether you are Christian, Buddhist, Muslim, Jewish, New Age, atheist or hold any other philosophies or faiths, you can work to live by your sexual ethics without self-punishment.

Consider Your Deepest Beliefs

How do they relate to sex? Meditate on the principles – not on the guilt, the shame and fear of failure, but on the high and noble values to which you aspire. Then when you are clear on what they are take a pen and paper and write down your commitments.

These can be as individual as you like. For instance, one person may choose, 'I will not have sex with anyone who I do not love and who I am not in a long-term relationship with'. Another person may choose, 'I will not have flings with anyone who is looking for more than casual fun and whose feelings I may hurt'. Promises to be faithful to your partner,

promises to be fair and ethical in your seductions, promises to be responsible about safe sex, to not fake orgasm, to give honest feedback in bed – all are expressions of your moral touchstones, a steadying guide to behaviour that will let you think well of yourself.

Once your commitments are made you are free to understand that guilt can be simply another emotion that floats through our minds, a distraction to be observed non-judgementally, much as any other. Make your resolutions to live as well as you can.

Live by those resolutions – and if you fail one of them, make what reparation you can, resolve to do better from now on and fix yourself once again in the present moment. You have done what you can as a human being to address morality, and you have no further need of guilt as a spur. Let your morality show in your actions, not in your self-hatred. You have done what you can, and will continue to do so. This is all that your conscience can ask. If negative feelings assail you, centre yourself in mindfulness. They will pass.

Performance Anxiety

Few things in this world are a greater self-fulfilling prophecy than performance anxiety, especially when it comes to pleasure. And we in the West, believers in achievement that we are, tend to think that to deserve our sexual freedoms we have to perform up to a certain standard. The desire to please one's partner is honourable and good – but few partners are pleased by a lover worrying themselves sick about whether they're Doing It Right. The more we worry in fact, the further we move away from our partners; blinded by anxieties, we become unmindful of their presence.

Erection Issues
For men the stresses of performance are considerable. A man expects himself to get an erection when desired, to stay hard with no fluctuations in tumescence throughout intercourse and to delay orgasm until the woman is satisfied.

The reality is that whilst most women enjoy erections, they are perfectly capable of being satisfied in many other ways – in fact whilst statistics vary, all agree that the majority of women climax through clitoral stimulation rather than deep penetration, and a man's mouth and fingers are certainly not subject to the vagaries of erection.

Many men know this but still struggle with feelings of inadequacy if their erection somehow fails to measure up. The central problem is this: most parts of our body are under our orders. If we want to wiggle our toes, we can wiggle our toes. The penis, however, is not under a man's conscious control. Getting an erection isn't a decision, and neither is ejaculation. Both are in effect symptoms of arousal – but not very indicative symptoms, as it's quite possible for a man to be aroused and have no erection to show for it. Even the great artist Leonardo da Vinci, infallible with his brush and his brain, remarked: 'The penis does not obey the order of its master, who tries to erect or shrink it at will, whereas instead the penis erects freely whilst its master is asleep. The penis must be said to have its own mind, by any stretch of the imagination.' Society expects a proper man to be in complete control at all times, and to have his penis, the outer emblem of his manhood, refuse to do as he wants can be devastating.

Female Arousal

For women the stresses can be equally strong but are sometimes less obvious. Orgasms are generally more elusive for women than men, and whilst women often don't like to admit it they can feel just as failed in their womanhood as men can in their manhood if they can't manage to have one. Women don't always lubricate on cue: whilst popular culture makes much of the G-spot and the multiple orgasm, women can sometimes feel inadequate if they can't seem to find the one or undergo the other. It's more possible for a woman to hide these issues: the clitoris and labia for instance can become 'erect' just as a penis can but the visual difference is far easier to miss.

The result is that intercourse can take place with a woman who is not aroused more easily than with a man who is not aroused – which can lead a woman to the destructive sense that her own arousal isn't really necessary for a sex life. Such a feeling can disconnect a woman from her body thoroughly, leaving her with the sense that if she were more feminine, more liberated, more sexy, she would be 'performing' easily, but as it is the whole business of pleasure is too unpredictable to rely on and a faked orgasm or a polite insistence that it doesn't really matter are the best way to go.

Staying In the Present

Just as destructive are the myths that arise when couples combine. Sex, the great myth goes, is easy if we are in love. If we love our partner, surely sex should work out all by itself?

This is foolishness of course. Even the most compatible couple in the world benefits from learning to dance together, from feeling out the rhythms and steps and graces of the other and learning how to move in time. The chances are that we will have dreamt of sex with a new partner, longed for it and pictured it before it happens. If we are unmindful, remembrance of past thoughts in which we imagined the future can distract us from the simple and joyous present.

With established couples another issue comes into play: familiarity. Can we reproduce the great moments of our past passions? And if not, does that mean the relationship has gone stale?

Rediscovering Each Other

In fact the past passions were probably when you were most in the moment. Sex in the early stages of a relationship is often dynamic and exciting precisely because the newness of the other person's body entices us into paying attention. But when we see it clearly, every moment is new. There is no second in this passing life that is quite like any other. The body may not be new to us, but this moment, its temperature and timbre and texture, is itself irreplaceable and changing and unique. The mistake is in waiting for the moment to take us over rather than integrating ourselves straight into it.

For both men and women this sadness and strain rests on the assumption that a proper person can have sex on cue, the right way, no matter what — and that this should happen by some kind of magic, like violins swelling in the background, with no contribution on our part. With this we assume that we don't have to listen to our bodies but that they have to listen to us – or that if we are going to listen to them, they will have to shout so loud as to deafen every other possible distraction. However, this is an unmindful attitude.

Becoming Absorbed

The truth is that for great sex there is no one physical requirement. Great sex is a matter of enjoyment, not of ticking boxes. A man may climax sooner than expected, but that's no reason to stop love-making. A woman's clitoris may not oblige, but she may thrill to glorious pleasure in her breasts and face. We love the sensation of orgasm, but when we think back over our really great sexual moments something else tends to stand out. However nice the orgasm, it was after all only

a few seconds – not enough to explain what made an encounter that great. What was usually so good was that we were totally absorbed in what we were doing, so caught up in pleasure that nothing else mattered to us, no past or future but just this, what we were feeling, what we were doing right then. Which is to say, sex had made us mindful.

We forget our anxieties in great sex. However, with mindfulness, we can also learn to let them go. We will be discussing love-making in more detail later, but the simple rule to remember is this: performance anxiety is a comparison between our ideas of what we should be and our fears of what we may be. Neither idea is a perception of what we are. To be anxious is to be distracted: with mindfulness we are too absorbed in perception to waste much time worrying.

When Performance Anxiety Strikes

Breathing is how we centre ourselves. If performance anxiety attacks us in the middle of love-making, we need to remember that anxiety is an emotion and emotions change. By all means we can be honest with our partners and let them know if we're nervous – and if we really don't like what we're doing, we can ask to stop. But if we have a moment of tension, it's also possible to treat it as a meditation.

Try This …
Without stopping what you're doing, close your eyes and focus all of your attention on your breath. Feel it coming in and out of your chest, and let your mind concentrate only on your breathing for a few moments. Anxiety tends to gather around the chest and diaphragm area: as you breathe you will feel the tension as if your ribs were expanding and contracting against it.

Keep breathing. Let go of any thoughts that may be in your mind such as: 'I can't do this', 'What if I can't please her?', 'What if I can't come?' Don't try to force them out of your mind – that is paying attention to them and keeping them present. Just let them fade away as you breathe. Forget about your thoughts and live in your skin, concentrating on nothing but sensation and the moment.

If the anxiety still doesn't pass and you're really uncomfortable, it's important to feel that you can call a halt. A partner who doesn't accept your right to ask for a time out doesn't respect your consent and should not be in your bed at all. If you need more time to centre yourself, then take a pause. But before you do that give the meditative moment a chance: you may be surprised at how quickly you come back into the mood when you give yourself permission to not be in it.

A Word About Pornography

To ask all people, especially men, to do without pornography in this internet age would be unrealistic. If you are in a relationship it's important to have an open conversation about the subject. Generally women are threatened by pornography for a number of reasons: they are afraid that their bodies don't compare with those of the performers, they are afraid that if their lovers 'see women as objects', they will have no concern for their feelings and they are afraid that their lovers will turn from them to the easier world of images. These are fears that sensitive lovers will respect and do their best to address honestly.

Two Principles

When it comes to pornography there are two basic principles of mindfulness. The first is this: if thoughts and images of pornography fill your imagination to the point where you stop noticing your partner, you need to take a step back, focus on the real world in front of you and address the fact that your sex life is long overdue a meditative makeover.

The second is that you owe some mindfulness to the people who perform for you. Pornography involves a considerable range of working conditions, from the grimly exploitative to the cheerfully clubbable; some performers are manipulated or coerced, some performers see it as a good way of enjoying their sexuality and making money. Try to find ethically produced porn. Check out the companies you buy from, see if the performers keep blogs or give interviews and do a little research. Whilst your interaction with a porn performer is necessarily limited, they have passed through your new life nonetheless, and whilst you don't need to care for them as you would a lover,

you should care about them as a
fellow human being and make sure
that you aren't giving your money
to people who have hurt them.

If You Decide to Watch …
When it comes to couples, some
conflict over pornography, some
agree and some even watch it together.
In a long-term relationship you will
need to find someone whose views
harmonize with your own.

For those who do choose to watch
pornography bear in mind that you're
handling explosive material. Neither the
male nor the female performers are cast
for the modesty of their endowments or

capacities, and modelling yourself on
them is a good way to cultivate the kind
of perfectionist self-hatred we have
been discussing. Most pornography is
shot to look good rather than to feel
good: real sex does not and need not
resemble it. There is a time to forget
and move past what pornography has
taught you and come back from the
unreal world of images to the real world
of your own body in your own bed.

For most people a little erotica is
an adjunct to a regular sex life, but it
should never be allowed to distract
you from your presence in the moment
or your interconnectedness with your
fellow human beings.

Self-Belief and Self-Love

Our place is in ourselves, in the moment of our existence. The judgement of others has no power to hurt us unless we internalize it, and if we are mindful of our own experience there is no need to. We know the motion of our bodies, our tastes and stirrings and yearnings as no one else can. Why would we let the fear of someone else's opinions take away from us that certainty of our own steady selves?

Trust in Yourself

The simplest explanation is this: the desire for sex is deeply bound up with the desire to satisfy. We are wired to the responses of other people, but in a culture where sex sells and ideals are everywhere the 'responses' of others are giving us misleading information. We see pictures of what we think other people want that echo in our minds so loudly we can't hear them telling us what they actually want. We

get bound up with performance and end up trying to please the invisible judge rather than our own partners, whether that judge comes from a locker room, a magazine or even a sex guide such as this one.

The last comment was not in fact a joke. Most of us are pretty good at castigating ourselves for failing to measure up to standards. If we're seeking to free ourselves from standards we believe to be too harsh and unfair, we sometimes simply find new standards to replace them – and then hold ourselves up to those standards as harshly as ever we did the old ones. If at any point you find you're measuring yourself against the comments in this book and feeling bad about yourself, come back to this page and read this sentence several times if necessary: you are fine, relax, take a deep breath and stop being so hard on yourself.

Let it Go

It's time to dismiss those judges, those self-proclaimed experts we never asked to burden us with their unsolicited advice. They are banned from our bedrooms.

Easier to say than to do, perhaps? If we try to do it with our conscious minds, undoubtedly. We cannot will a thought away. There is an old playground joke: 'Don't think about milk. What are you thinking of?' The answer is almost always 'milk', because trying not to think about something is a reliable way of calling it to mind. A few bad experiences of self-consciousness in the bedroom can have a similar effect. 'I hope I don't get worried about what he thinks of my stomach' will centre your attention uncomfortably on your stomach as sure as sure can be, and 'I hope I don't lose my erection' is as good as a cold shower for sending the penis into retreat. We know that certain thoughts are self-sabotaging – know it in our bones from all the times they've crept up and made our love-making less fun than we hoped it would be.

Finding Sexual Joy

However, deliberately deciding to banish the thoughts is only part of the solution. We need something else to put in their place. We need a deep absorption in the moment – and we also need a deep foundation of self-love. Guilt would have us believe that self-love is vanity, the sin of pride, arrogance that will ensure nobody will ever love us, but that is not what we are talking of here. Instead we need a secure and happy reconciliation with our own sexual selves as the absolute foundation of any sexual joy. This will be the subject of the next chapter, and the cornerstone of your journey.

When you think of sex what do you picture?

Perhaps you envisage two bodies entwined. The fact is, though, that another body is not the starting point for sex. Your own is.

We live in a world that treats self-pleasuring as a joke, an act of self-pollution or the last resort of a pathetic individual unable to attract a partner.

3. Beginning the Journey

To believe these cruel notions, however, is to resign responsibility for your own body.

Where do we feel arousal, pleasure and climax, if not in our own bodies? Where do we feel emotion, where do we experience the world, if not in our own selves? And if so, why not begin enjoying ourselves by ourselves? The idea that we must wait for a partner before we are entitled to bathe in sexual delight is, like so many destructive ideas, a plan of self-separation. It defers our experience to some moment in the future, although the means of enjoying it in full is here with us right now. We can begin whenever we choose – and if not now, when?

Start with Yourself

To be able to enjoy sensuality with another person we must be able to enjoy sensuality in solitude, just as we cannot dance with a partner before we have taught ourselves to walk. To take pleasure in satisfying our own bodies is natural. To do so mindfully is to immerse ourselves in joy.

We must travel the path on our own feet. It is time to re-enter our bodies.

Loving Kindness Exercise

Let us begin with an understanding: physical pleasure is one expression of joy, but it is founded in acceptance and openness. To feel pleasure we must feel compassion, to truly wish the best for ourselves and for others. Before moving on to sensual self-experience then, we should start by encouraging that spirit of acceptance on which all pleasure is based. The following exercise is called the *metta bhavana*, or 'the cultivation of *metta*' – a word that is best translated as 'loving kindness'. An ancient Buddhist meditation, it has tremendous power to heal and uplift us.

Settle Yourself into a Meditation

First get in a comfortable position. When you are ready begin by focusing your attention on yourself. Cultivate a sense of love and charity towards yourself. Dwell upon your good qualities: if bad ones come to mind, forgive them and return to your virtues

and achievements. Think of yourself as a precious and beloved individual for whom you want nothing but good. If it feels right to you, say this phrase in your mind: 'May I be well. May I be happy. May I be free from suffering.'

Expand Your Embrace

When you are filled with tenderness for yourself move your attention to a friend. For the purposes of this meditation it is best not to choose someone to whom you are related or sexually attracted: instead choose an acquaintance whose character you honour and whose well-being you care deeply for. Cultivate your love towards this person. Wish them joy. Let your love for yourself widen out to take them in. If you like, repeat the wishes you made for yourself for them.

Next move on to someone you have no special feelings about – the postman, perhaps, or someone you saw on the train. Feel a warm interest in them, their humanity, their lives, and hope that they may be filled with happiness.

After this think of someone you find difficult. Someone you hate and who makes your life a misery may not be the best choice, but find a person whom you usually find hard to like or think well of. Hold them kindly in your mind. Remember their fundamental humanity, their vulnerabilities and needs. Wish them health, happiness and freedom from suffering.

Finally gather all these people together. If you need to re-energize, focus on good feelings towards yourself for a while, then start to widen your love. Take in all the people you've thought of; then all the people in the street you're in; then everyone in the city, the country, the world, the universe, the present and the future. Let your well-wishing shine out in all directions, light and warm as the sun.

When you are ready return and centre yourself for a few moments before ending the meditation.

Treasuring Humanity

This exercise may be simple, but at its heart is the understanding that human beings are precious, that it is better for us to love than to hate, better for us to rejoice than to suffer. This is the foundation of mindfulness, of sex and of all truly joyous living.

When we accept that we deserve happiness, and recognise that we are amongst millions equally deserving of kindness, we cease to feel ourselves disconnected from humanity. We can treasure others because we treasure ourselves, and vice versa. This also encompasses love for all aspects of humanity – including of course our great capacity for sensual pleasure. Accepting our bodies and hearts, we are ready to enjoy them.

Redefining Self-Pleasure

The word 'masturbation' is an ungainly one with a number of possible sources, none of them very nice. It is possibly derived from the Greek *mezea*, meaning 'penis' (as if the activity was only for males) or the Latin *manus* and *turbare*, meaning 'hand' and 'disturb'. It has also been conjectured to come from *manu stuprare*, meaning 'defile with the hand'. Whilst the latter is most probably not correct, the fact that it was conjectured at all shows the problem.

Not Inferior and Not Wrong

For those who believe that sex is only for procreation this act has always been an issue. It is difficult to police – although this has not stopped people from trying, using gadgets to prevent access to the genitals or practising clitoral mutilation – yet it is instinctive to most people from childhood. Serving no purpose except to sweeten our own sensations, self-pleasuring lets us serve our bodies for our own delight, absorbed in a positive experience with our own thrilling flesh.

Others, meanwhile, tend to see self-pleasuring as a consolation prize, the poor second choice when we feel too unattractive to acquire a partner or when our partner is too busy for love-making. However, there should be nothing unsatisfying about self-pleasuring. Unless we believe the sole purpose of love-making is to prove we can persuade another person into bed with us, there is no reason to consider it an inferior experience. Whether alone or with a partner, we always seek to turn our bodies to delightful ends.

Love Yourself to Love Others

To pleasure ourselves is an act of introspective love-making. To expect humans to withold their pleasures and only wait upon the pleasures of others is to put all people in service to one

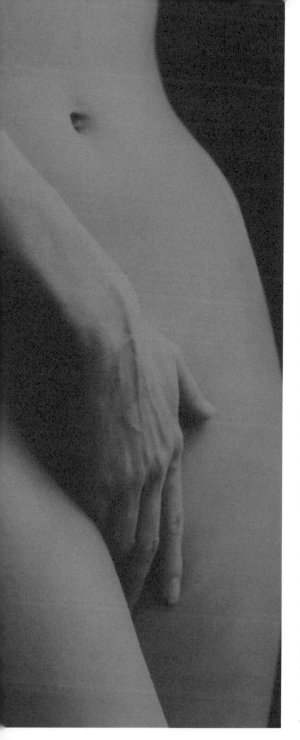

another, a harsh demand indeed. To shrug off self-pleasuring as a last resort is to cheapen a potentially wonderful experience to no purpose.

To judge self-pleasuring kindly we must believe that we are allowed happiness for its own good sake, to satsify ourselves for ourselves, to see ourselves as an end. Yet to strive to love and satisfy ourselves is sometimes decried as narcissism. It is indeed bad to be so preoccupied with our own interests that other people seem to us mere objects to be manipulated, but this is not the point of self-pleasuring.

Other people are the images of ourselves, our fellow creatures. To truly value and care for their flesh we must value our own – how can we honour our likenesses if we do not know how to honour ourselves? We are the human being we know best and have the most constant access to, and to love humanity we must begin with ourselves.

Sensuous Meditation Exercise

The purpose of this exercise is to introduce ourselves gently to our bodies as sensual vessels.

Get yourself into a comfortable meditation position. Begin by focusing on your breathing. Let the air into your lungs, let it out, let its rhythm settle you. Keep breathing mindfully until your body feels relaxed and clean.

When you are ready, keeping your breath calm, move your focus down your body. Become aware of your genitals. Rest your attention on them, peaceful and easy, ready to shiver and rise and give you pleasure whenever the moment is right. There is no need to shift on your chair or move around, although if a slight change in position makes the experience nicer, by all means change it. Just remain still and relaxed, taking in the sensations your genitals convey. Keep your attention balanced and your body poised, aware and rooted.

After a while spread your awareness to any other parts of your body that you find erotic. Feel the shape of your lips, the pressure of your buttocks on the chair or the weight of your breasts in your bra. Let a gentle smile come on to your face as your attention glows into the most sensitive parts of you. Again there is no need to move or touch. Just feel the experience of these organs, the outlines of your sexual self. Let your awareness become a map of your own eroticism, a glimmering overlay of pleasure that delineates where you can best rejoice.

If you begin to feel aroused, ride it. You don't need to do anything: just breathe easy, relax and enjoy it. Feel your body sing to itself like a struck bell. This is you, your flesh, your body's song. Smile a little and luxuriate in the sensation of just being yourself: a living sexual being.

Where Do Sexual Fantasies Fit into Mindfulness?

Logically it might seem that we should exclude sexual fantasies. Daydreaming, after all, stands between us and mindfulness: if we're picturing a sexual delight whilst walking down the street, we can forget where we are and become absorbed in our imaginations. Whether we are sitting on our cushions or meditating whilst walking through the streets, a sexual fantasy drifting into our heads would certainly be a thought we would strive to let go of, a distraction from the mindful moment. By this logic surely we should struggle not to fantasize?

The struggle would be a fruitless one. It's in the nature of human beings to fantasize about sex – and more importantly our fantasies are a rich and deep source of information about the core of our sexual selves. They may be out of place during a breathing meditation, but just as that meditation lets us experience the world around us, sexual fantasies are a direct map of the complex and fabulous world within us.

Accessing Our Imagination

Human beings are unique, and everyone is stirred by very different sexual experiences: to feel that we should all be alike is to set ourselves against reality. Some things we can discover a taste for by doing – but at the centre of our spirit is a sexual being with his or her own distinctive personality. It is by accessing that being that our most thrilling and profound experiences can be reached.

When it comes to listening to our fantasies there is a foundation of common sense – which is to say the intuitive wisdom that guides us through life. If for instance you always fantasize about lovers of the opposite sex, you are probably heterosexual: if you always fantasize about lovers of the same sex, you are probably gay. How else after all do we discover which way we're inclined if not by noticing our own attractions and fantasies? This obvious example serves to illustrate the importance of paying attention to what our fantasies tell us: when it comes to the big questions we already know to listen to our dreams.

Accept All Your Fantasies

Other issues can be more subtle. Are our fantasies rough or gentle, romantic or libertine, dark or light? Or all these things? Or none of them? The thing to remember is this: there is no such thing as an unacceptable fantasy. Your fantasies are yours, of you: to reject them is to reject yourself.

This does not mean you need to act on all of them of course. If you dream of kidnapping three women from a convent and keeping them as your naked slaves, it's definitely best

not to carry this out. However, the fantasy does tell you something interesting: that your sexual self longs to be powerful and forceful, and that your desires are towards women with an air of spirituality or innocence. Neither of these are bad things. Given the right partner, there are many ways of bringing at least the essence of this fantasy into your sex life, and whilst you pleasure yourself alone you harm no one.

As human beings aware of the humanity of others, we must never forget to treasure the rights and consent of our partners. Other people are not figments of our imaginations and we should not confuse the two. Nor should we grow so immersed in a fantasy that a partner becomes merely a screen to project on to. What is key is to identify the sexual essence that runs through our fantasies and find a way to enjoy it mindfully.

Sexual Fantasy Essence Exercise

Begin with a sensual meditation. Sit comfortably, feel yourself in your body and focus on the erotic parts of yourself so you are feeling sexy but relaxed.

Dive into Your Fantasies

In your receptive state take some time to consider your fantasies. Many of us have a repertoire of favourites that particularly excite us. Hold them in your mind for a moment – but rather than drifting off into replaying them, instead view them at a slight distance, as if you were hearing a strain of music.

What do they have in common? Are any details or moods essential? What is the feel of them?

Move on from your current favourites to become aware of your life as a long continuum. We are sexual long before we realize what sexuality is, right back into childhood. Consider all the fantasies you can ever recall having, as far back as your memories

go. Were there daydreams you found intriguing, early stirrings of sexual fascination? What were they like? Can you feel a line of connection between those and your current frissons? What about your adolescent dreams – how have they changed and developed?

It is in comparing our past and present sexual fantasies that we find the common touchstones, the base notes of our sexual imaginations. And it is in sounding those base notes that we resonate most deeply.

After you have experienced the weight and texture of your fantasies for a while, you may begin to get a shape, an idea of your fantasies' foundations. Don't worry if no immediate revelation strikes you. This is not a test but an exercise to be repeated at intervals throughout your life, a means of keeping in touch with yourself. Tease out what qualities you can: what you feel now is what you are seeking.

Visualize Your Erotic Self

When you are ready move to a
visualization. Your sexuality is a temple,
with golden ceilings and coloured
windows and all kinds of splendours.
In the centre of your temple stands
a figure, as glorious and gracious as
the temple itself. In your mind begin
to approach this figure.

    This figure is the self of your erotic
imagination, the actor who has played
so many roles in all your tableaux over
the years. These tableaux contain the
essential quality of your sexual self,
the identity that thrills you most
deeply to adopt. Who is this figure?
Picture his or her pose, dress and
aspect. Recognize that figure for who
he or she is: the sacred personification
of your sexual self, perfect, compelling
and your own. Let yourself fill with
acceptance for this figure, and with
admiration for its sensual freedom.
Convention, expectation, conformity
– none can touch it. It is simply its
natural, pure, untrammelled self.

Creating a Sacred Space

One can of course be mindful in any environment. When we accept that the world is simply what it is, no experience can shake our integration with it. However, our moods and arousal are sensitive to our environment, and when it comes to sexual pleasure we need not be ascetics. We should feed and nurture our senses as well as be at peace with them.

Setting Is Important

Creating a sacred space for your love-making can be a wonderful benefit. An uncomfortable room, crowded with reminders of our everyday lives, is not the most appropriate place for an ecstatic experience. When we create a sacred space we are showing ourselves how highly we value our sexuality, how deeply we are prepared to reward and to cherish it. If your sexuality is a fine jewel, it deserves a fine setting.

If you live alone you can create this space entirely to your own designs. If you already live with a partner, on the other hand, you will want to merge your sacred spaces together. There will be a discussion of this in the next chapter; however, begin by picturing your sacred space for yourself before you and your partner start sharing. If you discuss your thoughts of sacred spaces before doing the visualizations, you might modify your own vision to fit in with what you think your partner thinks he or she wants, and this will put you in dissonance with yourself. The most important thing is to be the real you, the inner, primal you: this is the gift you bring your lover, and the true substance is finer than any counterfeit. Complete your meditations on this subject before you and your partner adjoin your dreams. Knowing the sacred space inside yourselves, you and your partner can build together from firmer ground.

How Do You Create a Sacred Space?

If you have a spare bedroom or a room in the house you can afford to set aside, that's ideal. Such a room should be comfortable and beautiful, uncluttered but adorned with things that will focus your energy on the journey you are about to undertake. In it will be a bed, or a mattress on the floor, combined with everything you need to consecrate the atmosphere and make it ready for your love-making.

However, space can be at a premium and for many of us a spare room is simply out of our reach. What can be done in these circumstances? Can you manage a sacred space on a budget?

Of course you can. Sacredness is primarily a state of mind. When it comes to the practical details, there's a lot you can do to help things along.

Let's suppose that your home is small, and the only space available for comfortable love-making is your bedroom. This may also be the room where you keep your clothes, books and the odds and ends that don't go anywhere else, which is a useful arrangement but which gives the room a sense of being multipurpose rather than dedicated solely to the art of sex. How to sanctify such a place?

Making Your Bedroom Sacred

The first thing to do is ensure that the basics of the room are as comfortable as possible. Make sure it's clean and neat – not just for comfort but for practical reasons. If you want to try lying on the floor or curling up in a corner, there's nothing so off-putting as a pile of dust, so give the room a regular cleaning. If there's a stain on the ceiling that makes the place seem cheap and run-down, set aside some time to fix it. If you have a lot of clutter that distracts you, get some boxes and store things neatly. If the boxes put you off, find a beautiful

piece of fabric to drape over them, put an ornament on top, tape dried flowers to them – anything that makes them decorative rather than just 'in the way'.

If you can manage it, it's best not to have a television in your sacred space, because it enjoys the prestige of being one of the most distracting objects in the world. However, if there's nowhere else to put the television, find a cloth to cover it up, much as old-fashioned owners of a chattering parrot used to cover the cage when they wanted some peace and quiet.

Visualize Your Space

Picture this: you are a great king, a high priestess of the goddess, a magician or an empress or a white witch. You are a wise and beloved person of infinite wealth and boundless power who can order gold, lapis lazuli and emeralds, sandalwood and marble with a mere wave of your hand. Anything you want is yours.

Today your task is to plan the sacred room in which you will celebrate your sensuality. Wise and beloved as you are, you deserve nothing but the loveliest of rooms your heart can conjure: powerful and wealthy as you are, anything you can picture is within your easy reach. What will be in this room? A platinum dish to heat scented oils? A beautiful statue of Shiva dancing? An erotic frieze from the *Kama-sutra* covering an entire wall? Crystal glasses to drink from? An elegant fountain filling the room with the sound of trickling water?

Let your imagination run riot, and picture everything you'd like to have in this temple room of your mind. Be generous and unashamed: gorge yourself with luxury and excess.

Take the Essence of This ...

Now start thinking in practical terms. You may not be able to build your sacred room precisely to plans, but you are able to invoke it. Ask yourself this question: what was the thing in it you loved most? What detail most spoke to your sexual essence? Say that your imagined room has a life-size sculpture of a tiger in it, representing the grace and power you want your sexuality to channel. You may not be able to fit a tiger sculpture in your bedroom, but you can certainly find a small equivalent. Try your local shops, a gift shop, or check online. This will be your sacred object, the representative of the room of your imagination.

One or two items is plenty – too much clutter can be distracting – but take some child-like joy in finding your sacred objects. They don't need to be big or expensive: they just need to represent something that's special to you. If they're chosen with care, even small things can seem an abundance.

Keep these items together, along with the cloth you'll use to cover the television and perhaps a special bed-spread you'll lay down to consecrate your bed. Add to this some candles and scents, and any music you want to play to create a soothing background. When it comes to choosing music, you are your own best guide, but aim for something soothing and sensual, music that delights you without distracting you. Overly complicated lyrics or riffs may start making demands on your concentration, so your most sophisticated music is probably best listened to another time. Choose

something that settles your heart without entangling your ear. This will be your treasure trove, full of the objects that you'll use to set aside time and space for mindful love-making.

Attractive Colours and Textures

The bed, too, is important – it is, after all, where the majority of your love-making will take place. It should always be clean and comfortable. The sheets should be a texture that pleases your skin and in a colour that you like. Remember, too, that the bed need not be the only place for love-making – you may want to pile cushions in a corner or have a stool to sit on. Take advantage of what space you have.

When you enter your sacred space step in and prepare it calmly. Light candles, put on music and let yourself know that here you are safe and here you are precious. This is where your sensual self can come out to play.

The Question of Orgasm

The best time to begin reflecting on the question of orgasm is when we are alone with ourselves.

Too Much Pressure

Western ideas of sexuality can place both too much and too little focus on the climax. In the traditional encounter this is sex: man penetrates woman, man has orgasm, the end. If the woman doesn't come, it's still sex: if the man doesn't, it's an incomplete encounter. The imbalance of this is obvious, but as well as being unfair it puts too much pressure on both partners. If the man somehow doesn't manage an orgasm, he feels like a failure – although he's liable to feel a failure if he comes too soon as well. For the woman the pressure is on to sneak in an orgasm somewhere along the way, perhaps persuade her lover to satisfy her before they get down to the 'real' sex.

Which is to say the orgasm has a stopwatch attached. It's very hard to focus on the present moment when we're preoccupied with the thought, 'I need to have an orgasm right away if I'm going to have one', or 'I've got to stop myself from coming'. Both are fears of the future rather than observations of the present, treating the present as something we have to fight. A man trying to hold off his climax may even end up trying to distract himself with thoughts of boring things such as household chores – this is neither mindful nor fun!

Stop Watching the Clock

When making love within our own bodies, the important thing we need to learn, physically and psychologically, is how to relax about orgasm. As with most things about sex, this is something we have to learn by doing and time alone lets us build up experience.

Exercise: Riding the Climax Wave

Go into your sacred space. Light some candles, put on some ambient music if you like and make everything attractive. Prepare yourself by going into a short sensual position, then undress and make yourself comfortable. Begin pleasuring yourself. Rather than hustling towards orgasm as fast as you can, pleasure yourself as if this were a sensual meditation. Be present in your body, observing the sensations as they happen. Let the feelings of your sexual self possess you.

When you start to approach climax, carry on – but stop just before you tip over the edge. Breathe slowly and calmly, letting the sensation ebb away.

Begin pleasuring yourself again. Do not hurry to recapture the orgasm: just pleasure yourself, letting the feelings rise as they will. Your body is learning that a missed orgasm is not the end of the world – is not indeed the end of the love-making. Let the climax build again, and again let it go.

Bring yourself to the edge of orgasm at least three times before continuing on into climax – more if you're having a good time spinning things out. You will find as you do this that orgasm seems less and less like a train we must not miss or jump on too early, and more like what it is: a bodily response to stimulation that we can recapture.

If you accidentally do come during this exercise, don't worry. Just carry on. Most men have what is known as a 'refractory period' after orgasm in which they are unable to get another erection and the penis may be too sensitive to touch. If this is the case with you, again don't worry. Caress other areas of your body, enjoying and soothing yourself, letting your body see that you don't have to stop everything and give up the moment you climax. Pleasuring yourself can be a process of experimentation as much as a dependable source of release.

Other Exercises

As you continue your journey you may find it useful to try other variations of this exercise. Some examples:

• Pleasure yourself to the clock rather than to the climax. Set a radio alarm or CD player to begin some nice music five or ten minutes from now, and give yourself absolute permission not to come unless it happens naturally. After your time is up you can, if you choose, carry on to orgasm but let yourself experience a long moment where it is completely all right not to have one.

• Pleasure yourself to plateau. The period of intense anticipation before the climax begins is one of the most exciting experiences the human body can undergo. Stimulate yourself until you reach the plateau – and then stay balanced there, giving yourself enough to remain at that level but not enough to go over – as long as you can. (If you come down from the plateau without climaxing, remember the meditation on the previous page – pleasure can be recaptured.)

• Make a resolution that you will perform a sensual meditation for a full five minutes after an orgasm. Don't get up into meditation position – just remain where you were as still as possible. Stay in place and mindfully experience your body luxuriating in the afterglow.

These are simply examples, and as you explore your responses you may find other moments you want to expand or favourites you want to dwell upon. Follow your body's cues. When self-pleasuring becomes a meditation as much as a quick and furtive scuffle, all things are possible and many things become wonderful.

What About Sex Toys?

using a sex toy to pleasure ourselves than there is with using a spoon to eat ice cream. And those of us who don't want to visit shops selling sex toys can shop online for discreet and reasonably priced gadgets. The days of the dirty raincoat and brown paper bag are gone!

Vibrators – Good or Bad?

There is a persistent urban myth floating around that vibrators numb nerve endings and hence will destroy a woman's pleasure – an idea that speaks more to male fears of being replaced and to female guilt about enjoying themselves than to reality. Scientific studies have found that whilst the nerves can grow used to the vibration and hence become less sensitive to lighter stimulation, the effect is temporary and harmless, wearing off after a few days' rest. The clitoris is a resilient little organ

If self-pleasuring is time alone with ourselves, should we introduce inanimate companions?

For some people the idea of a sex toy is somewhat shocking, associated with sexual guilt or with seedy little sex shops on dingy back streets. In the case of guilt there is no reason to feel bad. Humans are a tool-using species, and as there's nothing wrong with sexual enjoyment, there's no more need to feel embarrassed about well designed to withstand impact, and the human body is a self-healing creation: there is no cause for alarm.

There's nothing medically or morally wrong with using a vibrator, and nothing particularly unmindful about it either – once again it's how we receive the sensation rather than the sensation itself that is mindful. Some women are unable to climax without one, and should certainly not be shamed out of their rights. However, if you can come by a variety of methods, it's a good idea to vary them to avoid getting into a rut and denying your body the panoply of different pleasures it's capable of experiencing: getting into a rut with any method can lead to the absent-mindedness of routine. Pleasuring yourself with your hands alone can feel more intimate than using a vibrator, and intimacy with ourselves is definitely something to cultivate.

Variety is Best

The same applies to other sex toys. If you find yourself growing overly dependent on a particular one, it's time to take a step back. Too much reliance on an old stand-by can spring from fear and worry that you might not be able to come. This can lead you to reach for the predictable thing rather than experimenting to see what will happen. If this is happening to you, the problem is with your anxieties rather than your nerve ending. Some sensual meditations and relaxed, no-pressure-to-come self-pleasuring will help you to relax and rediscover faith in your own sexual capacity.

If, however, a toy is an occasional adjunct to a happy and varied sex life, there's no reason to abstain. Sex toys can be a delightful addition to the treasure-trove of your sacred space, and denying ourselves extra pleasure is a waste.

Conclusion

Self-pleasuring is not a phase to pass on from. It is an endlessly unfolding map of our sensuality, a refreshment and a guide to ourselves.

Self-Pleasuring Myths

The idea persists in some people's minds that because self-pleasuring usually begins in adolescence and is the steady resource of many a teen not yet ready to navigate the wild and scary seas of romance, we should 'grow out' of self-pleasuring, just as we generally grow out of fighting with our parents about curfews and clothes, and considering anybody over the age of thirty decrepit. But this is far from the truth. Teenagers do not pleasure themselves because they are teenagers; they pleasure themselves because they are human beings. We do not stop being human when we turn twenty, and neither are we required to stop pleasuring ourselves.

As we continue the journey it is important to remember that pleasuring yourself is no less sacred than pleasuring a partner. Neither is it an infidelity. Yet if we exhaust ourselves self-pleasuring until we have no energy left for our partner, that's a problem as it suggests an emotional disconnection between the two of you. Done mindfully, however, self-pleasuring is an exploration of our own bodies and thoughts. By doing so we keep in touch with our deepest sensuality.

To be unselfconscious when making love with another we need to feel safe in our own skins. A consistent experience in taking pleasure with ourselves energizes and strengthens us to know that our bodies are not empty barrels we must scrape to dredge up scraps of joy, or old engines rattling and blasting off at unpredictable moments. We are responsive creatures, able to feel more than our worries would have us believe. An open mind is the beginning of this: to it we can add an ever-increasing storehouse of experience.

Pleasure for Pleasure's Sake

The purpose of these experiences is not to burden ourselves with reminiscences and standards to live up to. A great session of self-pleasuring on a Monday is fine if on Tuesday we are able to think, 'I know I can feel great pleasure, whether it happens or not right now': however, if on Tuesday we think to ourselves, 'I must try to feel what I felt yesterday or I'll be backsliding', we are punishing ourselves with thoughts of the past and fears of the future again, and we need to come back to where we are now. The point of pleasure is always pleasure, not the creation of new sticks with which to beat ourselves.

Pleasure is felt in our own bodies, and we use our own bodies to seek it. With a steady foundation of love for

ourselves, we become non-judgemental, and happy for others to be happy because we are learning that joy is a wellspring, not a finite resource. There is always enough to go around, because we create it ourselves.

'The reduction of the universe to the compass of a single being, and the extension of a single being until it reaches God—that is love.'

—Victor Hugo, *Les Miserables* [8]

What is more amazing than a lover? When attraction to another human being moves us the universe can shift. A desired person becomes magical, their skin,

4. *Appreciating Your Partner*

their voice, their very socks resonating with light. We look, see and are astonished. What we see when we look with desiring eyes is a glimpse of the miracle that is a human being. Every person in the world is an astonishing triumph against the odds. The chance meeting of their ancestors stretching back across the eons, the union of one egg with one of many millions of possible sperm, have produced this person – this one and no other. Surrounded by other folks every day, we generally grow used to them, but desire can lift the veil … and we see, with sudden passion, the impossible preciousness of a human life.

Mindfulness For Two

Yet miscommunication, insecurity, mundanity, can all do their work. To look through the eyes of love is one thing – but how do we carry our mindfulness into a life with another person? Partnership demands kindness and courage: its challenges offer us daily opportunities for small acts of heroism that can keep the flame burning. When we journey with another by our side, the tests and the rewards can be extraordinary.

Relationships

What kind of relationship should we be in? The answer will vary from culture to culture and person to person. Sexual liberation, as we understand it in the West, traditionally means the freedom to have a lot of partners. At the other end of the spectrum many followers of Tantra are advocates of monogamy, strongly believing that the foundation of trust necessary to spiritual sex is best achieved in a committed context. Many people end up somewhere in between, and many more just aren't sure.

How Many Partners?

There are certainly some advantages to monogamy. Safer sex in this era of AIDS is one of them: whilst it's possible and wise to use condoms, dental dams and so on if one has multiple partners, the risks remain at their lowest for monogamous couples. Also sex, when experienced deeply and openly, can stir up strong feelings. It is easiest to be vulnerable with someone we know we can confide in. The exercises we will be discussing in the following chapters are best practised with a partner who understands their significance: if sexual discovery is a journey, committed relationships are the best way of ensuring you and your partner are travelling in the right direction.

However, we are at our happiest when following our own natures, and for some people monogamy simply does not feel like the right answer for them. Open relationships or polyamorous commitments to more than one partner at a time have been known to work better for those who feel this way – and a single person mindful of his or her own sexuality and who is careful of his or her own safety is certainly free to enjoy a fling with a charming stranger.

The most important thing when it comes to relationships is honesty. You need to be mindful enough of your own feelings to be clear what works for you, and you must be respectful enough of others' feelings to give and receive communication, to refrain from manipulating or coercing them and above all to keep any promises you make, explicit or implicit.

A Few Boundaries

As an aside some books advise spicing up your love life with exhibitionism or public sex. This book advises against it. In any ethical sexual encounter it's crucial that every participant has given their informed consent, and that includes people who may stumble upon you. Bystanders have not consented to be involved in our sex lives. What we must remember is that we are not only in a relationship with a partner, but with humanity. Both need to be treated with respect. We can glory in our sexuality, but we must also be tender of the boundaries of others.

As we reveal ourselves to each other we may discover issues of compatibility: not every couple is perfectly matched. In cases of mismatch, mindfulness is as much a protection as a spiritual or sensual practice. Keeping an awareness of our own feelings, we become more clear that how we feel is simply how we feel, and that we cannot change it to please someone. Some compatibility issues can be resolved with mutual respect and tenderness. If they cannot, a mindful relationship with our own sexuality can be the best support we need to enable us to step back and decide that it's better to be alone than in a relationship that isn't going to work.

Ultimately there is no 'right' kind of relationship. There are only relationships that work for everyone involved and relationships that don't. The important thing is to know ourselves well enough to choose a relationship we can live well in.

Inviting Your Partner In

You and your partner have decided to deepen your connection and want to use mindfulness to do it. So how do you begin?

As the previous chapter explained you will be well advised to explore and strengthen your connection with yourself first. That way the gift of self you offer your lover will be in prime condition. Meditating together can be wonderfully companionable, as can discussing your shared experiences.

Sharing a Space

If you live with your partner, you will want to create a sacred space together. The process of visualization and preparation described in the last chapter is the same: the difference is that you share the process of creating it. When you have your sacred room fully planned describe it to your partner. Let him or her in on your dreams; laugh in delight at each other's glories. When it comes to finding objects to represent you, make it a shared trip with your partner, an adventure in which the two of you hunt down treasures together – or perhaps an opportunity for giving gifts if you feel confident enough of each other's tastes.

Opening Up

The same applies when it comes to sharing fantasies. This can be a scary process – we worry that the other will think us perverted or sentimental, foolish or weird. There is something especially vulnerable about exposing so secret a part of ourselves. Whilst we need not go into precise detail if we're truly uncomfortable, it is important for a good connection that we can at least express the essence of our fantasies. This essence is the key to our sexual self, the self we long for our partner to recognise and embrace.

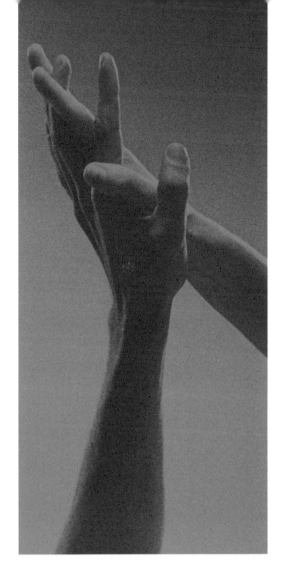

honest about them. Learn all you can about your partner's sexual self. Who knows? He or she may have been your perfect complement all along.

When we first start to discover ourselves in solitude it can be a little difficult to welcome someone else over the threshold. We've only just worked out where everything is, we had to be alone to do it and what if he or she starts messing everything up? Inviting your partner in can be an act of great trust, especially when we're just learning the benefits of solitary reflection. A good partner is willing to respect the other's space, though, and to value just how great a gift that invitation is.

Likewise one person opening him- or herself to another honours both, and when our partner opens him- or herself to us we must always receive the gift tenderly. Once we have established a bond of trust, revelations become easier and more delightful.

Listen with an open mind, confess without shame. To reach sexual harmony with each other we have to know who the other truly is. Sharing sexual fantasies can raise issues of compatibility – but those issues will always be there. The key is to be

Making Love to Each Other's Feelings

The first step in the journey together is a simple one: helping each other to love ourselves. There's more than one kind of love-making in the world. This writer once met a bishop who described doing the ironing as a way of making love to his wife, and this method sits at the foundation of any good sexual connection – making love to each other's confidence. As we can pleasure each other's bodies, making them relaxed and content, so too, we can satisfy each other's feelings.

Inspiring That Confidence
Praise your partner generously, frequently and honestly. This last point is just as important as the first two, because it's essential to trust. There's absolutely no point telling your boyfriend he has an amazing six-pack if a quick glance downwards will inform him otherwise. Likewise assuring your girlfriend she's a long-legged gazelle when she's less than 150 centimetres (5 feet) tall will not inspire her with confidence in your judgement. Your partner has to be able to believe you, otherwise your sincere compliments will fall on sceptical ears, which isn't good for anyone. On the other hand your honest admiration is a precious gift. You have something amazing you can offer your partner – a view through the eyes of love.

Seeking Out the Positive
Try this: take a feature that your partner isn't so confident about and tell them why you like it. Rather than arguing that it's not so bad, really – which seldom helps and can feel like you're invalidating their opinions – come at it from another angle, surprising them with your own perspective. If your girlfriend thinks her thighs are too fat for example, rather than telling her that they're not,

try telling her instead that you love the feel of their soft silky skin, the delicate way the flesh moves when you touch it, the tempting strokeable curves. If your boyfriend thinks his hair's too thin, rather than shrugging it off spend some time praising his fine brow, the excellent shape of his head, the handsome set of his shoulders that makes the receding hairline look so thrillingly masculine. Find what you like in that feature and make sure your partner knows about it.

Of course one of the nicest things about this attitude is that it's reciprocal. Such things are excellent karma: in giving compliments one is repaid not only in words but in seeing our partner's happiness. It's also good to hear ourselves speak positively. The more you do it, the more you will find your attitude to beauty is loosening up. You'll begin looking for things to admire rather than looking for faults, and once you start doing that the whole world becomes a divine place. Reassured and reassuring, your heart starts to open to the simple but profound idea that you can find loveliness everywhere.

When your partner compliments you, your first impulse may be to contradict him or her. Humility is a great virtue if it means accepting the world and other people for what they are rather than arrogantly demanding reality complies with your demands. But, there are a lot of false ideas about humility and one of them is that a properly modest person always insists that he or she is unattractive. If you find yourself having this impulse, don't put yourself down for it. Just let the thought drift into your mind, notice that it's there and don't worry about it. It's just a reflex. Let it go and focus on the gift you're giving your partner: the glad acceptance of his or her admiration.

Self-Pleasuring in a Relationship

The myth persists in many places that once we find a partner, self-pleasuring should go and that if it doesn't, it's a sign that something's wrong. This idea has led to many hurt feelings and frustrations. At the root of it lies the twin fears that our secret doubts about ourselves are true – that we aren't enough for our partners because we couldn't be enough for anyone – and that self-pleasuring is somehow dirty or perverted. Neither fear is true. Self-pleasuring is how we keep in touch with our own body, making a gift of it to us as an informed one.

When we honour our right to make love with ourselves, we become open to something else – watching each other as we pleasure ourselves. This does not mean we have to watch each other every time – an arrangement that could quickly become inconvenient for all concerned – but watching a partner pleasure him or herself is one of the best, as well as the most fun, ways of discovering what strokes and rhythms and touches are preferred.

Allowing ourselves to be watched, too, is a wonderful way of letting our inhibitions melt. To let another person see us in the most private of moments builds trust and intimacy in a unique way. Our lover sees us, absorbed and exposed in our own pleasure, and accepts us. When we are enveloped in our lover's presence in such a moment, we know that we are truly welcomed for who we are.

Self-consciousness about our own pleasure is a great hindrance to sexual happiness. Learning to be comfortable in the presence of another is a lovely way to get past this self-consciousness and understand that there is truly nothing wrong with enjoying ourselves.

Recovering a Sense of Wonder

Because we see them every day we sometimes forget what an amazing thing the human body is. Consider the part of your lover you'll encounter almost everywhere you look: the skin. Just 6.5 square centimetres (1 square inch) contains 71 metres (78 yards) of nerves, 1,300 nerve endings, 65 hairs and 9.5 million cells. The mind can hardly take in such complexity, such dazzlingly vast numbers. Yet even without our understanding it, the body works quietly away, every single second of our lives, renewing itself, repairing itself, a living and regenerating sculpture that carries our souls through this world.

When we see our lovers through mindful eyes this sense of wonder can refresh itself, deepening our attraction and reminding us that the miraculous is all around us. There is nothing ordinary in this world that is not extraordinary, looked at with open eyes.

Focusing Exercise

Make a small circle with your thumb and forefinger and place it somewhere on your lover's body. That defines your area of attention: now you can remove your hand – you'll have better things to do with it momentarily.

Breathe calmly and focus your perceptions on that small part of your lover. Study the grain of his or her skin and the way the hair contrasts with it. Look to see if you can observe any blood vessels, any scars, any movement of the muscles. Let your energy be absorbed in that small area. Now try stroking it with your fingertips. What's the texture like? And the temperature? How does it respond to your touch?

Finally study it with your mouth. Feel all the fine details your sensitive lips can perceive. Can you smell the scent of your lover? What can you hear? Is there a special taste?

As you focus your eyes on the small circle you may find that the rest of your body warms with awareness of the rest of your lover. Don't try to block this out. Seen with microscopic vision your lover's body is a vast continent, an inexhaustible landscape of fascination. Let your attention to the particular draw you into a mindful awareness of the whole. This one can be a good way to enjoy your lover when they're asleep as well as when they're awake. If they're still sunk in dreams and you're too considerate to disturb them, a meditation on whatever part of them you can see above the covers – the curve of a shoulder, the back of the neck, a stray foot – can keep you happy and fascinated whilst they finish their doze. They may be pleasantly surprised at your mood when they finally do open their eyes.

Eye Gazing

The eyes, so the saying goes, are the windows of the soul, and the bond we can make through simple eye contact can be overwhelming.

In everyday life we seldom meet other people's eyes for more than a glance. Children are told, 'It's rude to stare' and an insecure person may bluster, 'What are you looking at?' It's generally true that the only people who gaze are lovers and babies.

Looking straight into the eyes is an ancient Tantric ritual: scientists today believe that gazing can release oxytocin (often known as the 'love hormone'), which is also released through touch, and which helps bond us together. A gaze can be as good as a caress in bringing us closer to our lovers.

Gazing Exercise

Sit yourself opposite your lover and bring your faces a comfortable distance apart. Simply look into each other's eyes. Breathe deeply and calmly, centre yourself mindfully and gaze. After a few seconds you may have the urge to look away – after all most of our lives we have been told not to do this. But whatever feelings arise in you keep looking. Hold each other's hands if you want, and just look into each other's beautiful eyes.

After five minutes – or more if you like – move towards each other. Don't break your gaze and turn away; instead flow gently into each other's arms and hold each other. This is what the Tantric writer Margo Anand calls the Melting Hug – an embrace preceded by eye gazing – and is a wonderful way to renew your connection and to end or begin an intense experience.

Eye gazing is not an exercise to do only once. It is a meditation you can return to when you want to feel your connection with your beloved. Simple and ancient, it grounds us in each other.

What's This Talk of Ritual?

When we say the word 'ritual' to a Westerner it can sound alarmingly esoteric. Does this mean chanting and bowing, odd performances we must struggle to get our heads round? Does it mean subscribing to peculiar doctrines that sound nice but don't convince, which try to make us believe that we can produce improbable effects by saying magic words and drawing magic symbols?

Far from it. Ritual is a universal human instinct, one of the ways we automatically locate ourselves in relation to the most important parts of our lives. We all have rituals associated with sex. Once we understand this the concept of rendering sex sacred becomes much more approachable.

What for instance is the tradition of a romantic candlelit dinner if not a ritual? Picture an anthropologist from an alien planet describing it. Despite having working electric lights, we plunge ourselves in darkness, light flames, set out special foodstuffs to consume together, often accompanied by music. All of this is ritual behaviour. It feels normal to us because it's familiar, but that in itself shows how comfortable with ritual we can be.

We are perfectly comfortable imbuing particular objects with ritual significance too. Scientists puzzle over whether there's any chemical basis for the supposed aphrodisiac qualities of oysters or asparagus, but the answer is right before us – these are foods that have a ritual symbolism. We don't necessarily believe that oysters contain some sex-provoking chemical. Many lovers have ordered them not because they believe that the oyster meat will entice their desired one, but because they understand that their beloved will recognise the gesture for what it is – an invocation of lust using the appropriate object. It is not a question of believing the untrue: it is simply a question of using certain things to send a message to ourselves and to our partners that we want a certain ambience to be created.

Ritual Is All Around Us

When we understand the symbolic value of ritual we see it everywhere. What is our tradition of clinking champagne glasses with a lover – or a prospective lover – if not a form of salute, a way of honouring him or her? What is a gift of roses or chocolates if not a symbolic appeal to our lover's senses? What is calling a particular tune 'our song' if not imbuing it with ritual significance? Many, if not most, long-established couples have their own rituals, be it a particular meal, a familiar double-act joke or an anniversary. Some may be traditional, some eccentric, but all are instinctive reaches towards ritual, and all can be performed with mindfulness and joy.

There's no need to fear ritual or worry that it's impossible for us. We already do it.

We can if we like choose to research and perform rituals from Eastern traditions. There is no reason not to, and they can be deeply rewarding. However, we should not feel obliged to use the rituals of another tradition. As we can see when we look clearly our own traditions provide an abundance to choose from. As with most things in sex choosing the right ritual objects comes down to what works best for you.

When it comes to mindfulness, performing the same act more than once can be a fascinating study in how the world changes and our own feelings shift. Rituals are a way of touching base and creating continuity. Understood in its simplest terms, a ritual is a way of telling our minds that what we're about to do is special and worth its attention.

Bath Ritual

The idea of making oneself ritually clean is common to many religions: to shed impurities and render oneself new again is a sacrament. Enchantingly enough, bathing is also a lovely sensual pleasure. Combine the two and you have a perfect ritual for lovers.

In addition to the symbolic value of cleanliness, homo sapiens is one of those animals that loves to play in the water. From trips to the beach to spas and steam baths, people throughout the ages have been drawn to splash and soak whenever they want to treat themselves. Enjoy a bath, and you are partaking of one of the oldest pleasures in history, sensually uniting yourself with the whole of humanity.

On a more practical level you are also making your skin clean, soft and smooth – an excellent preparation for love-making – and warming your muscles into relaxation. Tension is

no good for sex, and it's good to smell and feel as delicious as possible when entering the arms of your lover.

Setting the Scene
Ensure your bathroom is clean and comfortable before you start – squalor and mess are nothing to include in a ritual. Prepare cosy towels in advance, set out candles and put on some music you both like. Fill the bath with hot water and add oil, perfume or bath bombs to scent it. If you don't have a bath, a shower is fine. Get some delectable soap to make the experience feel special. Make sure the room is warm, not forgetting that you'll be chillier when you get out of the bath than when you got in and you don't want to end the ritual by shivering and dressing as fast as possible.

Begin by brushing your teeth to make sure you're clean all over. If you like to shave your legs or face, it's best to do

this earlier on because stray hair can make the water less appealing and shaving is a solitary activity – and not usually the most fun either. Be as ready as possible before you get in the bath.

Take Your Time

Get in together and bathe each other slowly, lingering on each part of your lover's body. Luxuriate in the heat and the silky feel of the water: wrap yourselves around each other, slippery with suds. Let your troubles and anxieties be washed away with each stroke: you are cleansing each other of distractions and problems. Take your time and enjoy each other.

When you are finally ready to get out, dry each other off gently, as if you were polishing a statue of gold. Honour each other's bodies, clean and refreshed together.

Pre-love-making Ritual

Just as dinner and a film can be a way of preparing for a good-night kiss, rituals in established relationships can be a fine way to consecrate our evening to love-making. Whilst repetition can be soothing, it is also good to vary rituals so we don't become too bored. The following ritual is loosely based on Tantric traditions, but the origin is not the important thing for our purposes. What matters is what best centres you and your lover in a vibrant, safe sexual space. You can shape your rituals to suit yourselves, adapting and adding to them as you learn what helps you best.

A Little Warm Up

Begin by making your sacred space ready and bathing together. When you enter your sacred space do a short meditation together, settling into your bodies and clearing your minds. After this you may choose to do a little physical exercise to warm yourselves up. Yoga is good but ordinary stretches are also fine if you prefer. An alternative exercise is dancing together, a charming way to get each other interested and introduce some fun to the proceedings.

After this begin honouring each other by massage. Traditionally the woman is massaged first. This has the advantage of giving her a longer warm-up time, which she may need, and is no hardship for a man who delights in handling his beautiful partner. Perform some sensual massage, adding words of appreciation and devotion, praising the other's femininity or virility, pouring your attention into honouring his or her sexual self in all its glory.

A Small Taste

If you choose you can add this next stage: ritual food and drink. Set them out on a little altar with candles, ready to taste. The selection is up to you. There should not be more than a small taste of everything because you don't want to weigh yourselves down. Tantra suggests wine, representing fire; meat, which represents animal life; fish, representing the sea; cereal, representing the earth; with sexual union at the end, which represents cosmic energy. Westerners may feel more comfortable with familiar symbols of sensuality such as chocolate, representing romance; bread, which represents the earth and reality; salt (or a salty snack) to represent cleanliness; a childhood candy to represent innocent sensuality and so on, perhaps even including personal favourites to show your participation in the ritual. Finish with something to make your mouth feel clean and your breath pleasant – a quick chew on some sugarless gum or a breath mint are both practical substitutes to the traditional cardamom seed. You can even brush your teeth if you bring in toothbrushes and a glass, as long as that doesn't feel too clinical. When you have finished your ritual, you have prepared yourselves for love-making – a subject for the final chapter.

To a couple used to 'quickies' this may seem like a long process and some mindfulness may be called on to ride out feelings of impatience or anxiety. Breaking off to meditate for short periods during the ritual is fine. Nor need we go through the process if we are suddenly overwhelmed by passion. A lover's pounce is one of the great moments of a sexual relationship, and it would be a great loss to deny ourselves that because we felt we needed to go through a ritual every time. But life can encourage us to forget the sacredness, the extraordinariness, of our sexual bond with a partner, and it's good sometimes to touch base and remind ourselves of this.

Kissing

The sensual glide of lip over lip, the intimate touch of tongue against tongue, is one of the ultimate symbols of lovers' closeness. For most of us a kiss is our first real sexual intimacy: a kiss is how we symbolize the completion of a marriage ceremony. There is something eternally new about kissing, a freshness filled with possibilities. With a kiss we rejoice the completion of one phase of life and the opening of a new.

Find the Time

Make some time in your relationship to do nothing but kiss. Such a time will be far from repetitive if you remember that kissing is more than just the press of mouths or a quick dart with the tongue. Try kissing by moving only your lower lip over your partner's mouth, or by licking only his or her upper lip. Find a rhythm and tap just the tips of your tongues together over and over in greeting. Suck at each other's mouths

as if drawing out each other's spirits: have a playful contest of tongue against tongue as if matching swords. Drop a string of featherlight kisses on your partner's lips, mouths closed and delicate. Draw your lover's lower lip gently through your teeth, teasing with tender care. When we kiss with mindful creativity we are enacting an infinite range of caresses in a single sensitive area, an erotic form of seeing the world in a grain of sand.

Never mind 'French' kissing – whatever nationality you are that is the kissing you are doing. Rather than dividing kissing into the closed mouth and the open mouth, the tongue and the non-tongue, free yourself to discover that there are no categories of kissing, only the movement of mouth on mouth. This is one of the most mutual of all the sexual acts, a means for a woman and a man to enter one another and open up to one another as mirrors rather than complements. Kiss your lover and you meet your match.

Another exercise can be added to kissing: breathing together. Sit with your body pressed up against your lover and seal your mouths together. Let your breaths fall into rhythm, breathing into each other's lungs: as one lover exhales the other inhales, then vice versa. Breathe together slowly and deeply, not touching tongues or moving your lips but just drinking in the same air. This is an exercise that should last a minute: there will be enough oxygen to sustain you for more than a few breaths, but obviously stop if you start to feel suffocated. This embrace is a shared act of mindful breathing, an astonishingly intimate act of mutual meditation.

Kiss Everywhere

Kisses of course need not be confined to the lips. Try kissing your lover all over the face, moving over the

cheeks, grazing the eyelids, sucking the tip of the nose and nibbling the ears. Such an activity takes the face, the part of ourselves we most associate with our personality, and graces it as an erotic whole.

Making out is not just for teenagers. The kiss is our deepest gesture of love, of greeting, an act of welcome as much as an act of sensuality. Its joys are as much emotional as physical. Kiss your lover's spine, the nape of the neck, the soles of the feet: taste the fingertips, burrow your tongue between the toes. The possibilities of kissing are as limitless as the possibilities of love itself.

Conclusion

As we explore the many ways we can be with our partner, the importance of communication will be paramount.

Yes, But vs Yes, And

Actors sometimes play a game called 'Yes, But/Yes, And', which you can find useful to try. In 'Yes, But' one partner makes suggestions whilst the other always begins a reply with 'Yes, but'. For example, 'Let's make a cup of coffee' could bring the reply, 'Yes, but I'm not thirsty'. This can lead to, 'Let's go for a walk, then'. A response could be, 'Yes, but I'm tired'. 'We could take a nap for a while' leads to, 'Yes, but that would be boring'. And so on. It is remarkable how frustrating this game becomes.

In 'Yes, And' the reply changes. 'Let's make a cup of coffee' leads to 'Yes, and let's have some biscuits with it', then 'Yes, and we could bake them ourselves', followed by 'Yes, and let's

bake a pie whilst we're at it'. In the latter game total strangers can end up pledging each other eternal love or a trip to the moon – agreeing with one another is very energizing.

Sometimes of course we don't agree, but it is good to remember the lessons of these games. If we need to speak with someone, it is best to discuss constructively and not block everything they say. The following exercise is a charming one for cultivating a sense of affirmation between you.

Communication Exercise

Sit opposite each other, looking into each other's eyes. The first lover speaks a sentence, something true and simple, such as 'The sky is blue' or 'My name is Antoine'. The second lover looks into his or her eyes and replies, 'Yes'. The first lover speaks their sentence again, the second lover again replies, 'Yes'. Carry on this conversation for five

minutes, letting whatever emotions wash through you enter your tone, and letting your lover ground and accept you with his or her steadfast, positive reply. The game is not complex but it can provoke surprisingly strong feelings: as long as you anchor each other, you are securing your bond through speech.

Staying Trustful and Mindful

As long as we are together we entrust our lovers with our hearts and accept the care of theirs. With regular meditation and a mindful sense of self, we will always remain individuals who freely choose to journey together. We will never melt into one entity, nor would we want to. Whoever we love, we are always ourselves. To be with another person is an act of balancing, honouring ourselves and him or her, never forgetting the respect and mindfulness due to both. This balancing act will always wobble a bit: mindfulness helps to steady ourselves again. As with every other aspect of life perfectionism is a recipe for a lot of unhappiness, and we understand each other best when we recognise each other for the fallible, wonderful people that we are.

The art of massage is one of the oldest healing methods in the world: one that has lasted through centuries of theories, mistakes and revelations. Even Hippocrates, the father of medicine, decreed that a good physician must be skilled in 'rubbing'. Across different cultures, the comforting experience of massage is to be found everywhere.

5. Sensual Massage

Between lovers massage has a special role. The intimacy we experience lets us use this noble art for everything from soothing a sore shoulder to coaxing out a sexual frenzy. Massage lets us know our lovers' bodies in a way that is literally more than skin-deep. When we rub a lover's back we are honouring not just the visible flesh but the very muscles and bones. When we massage a lover's genitals we are dedicating ourselves to his or her pleasure with profound nurture and absolute attention.

Different schools of massage teach a variety of different techniques, but the core principle when massaging a lover is simple: we must think with our hands. To perform a series of moves according to some mental diagram is unmindful: we must feel with our fingers the textures and resistance and yielding of our lover's flesh, and let that be our guide.

Take Your Lover's Cues

Similarly we must learn to read our lover's responses – the stiffening of the body when we press too hard, the moan of relief when we hit the right spot – all are signs that show us how best to rub our lover into happiness. Massage is physical, intuitive and irreplaceable.

Understanding the Basics

We must always remember that we are massaging an individual, not a model or a photograph in a book. Everyone has their own preferences, their own tight spots, favourites and touch-me-not places. An understanding of humanity is a fine groundwork.

To massaging hands the human body is a series of layers. Overlaying bone is muscle, a firm and fibrous tissue that tends to get tight, and it is the muscles that you will be rubbing. Overlaying the muscle is fat, the protective coating we are so self-conscious about. The thickness of this layer will obviously vary from person to person: fat is soft and contains fewer nerves, and is the layer you will be pressing through to reach the muscle. The idea that massage promotes weight loss is a myth: it can, however, let people experience their body as cherished, an essential experience for anyone

displeased with themselves. The subcutaneous fat is covered by sensitive and responsive skin.

Lubricant

To avoid hurting the skin a full massage usually calls for some kind of lubricant. Oil is often preferred because it moisturizes and flows smoothly: as long as you will not be using a condom or protective gloves later, this is your best choice. If you will be, talcum powder can be a good alternative, or you may seek out water-based lubricants to massage the genitals, though these tend to dry out quickly, so silicone-based may be preferable.

When massaging skin first pour a little oil into your cupped hand and rub it between your palms to warm it up. Spread it over the skin with flowing sweeps. How much you use will depend on your partner: drier skin absorbs more, and hairier skin needs more lubrication so the hair doesn't snag painfully on your hands. The skin should feel smoothly oiled rather than greasy.

When adding oil it is nice to reflect on the duality of the act you are performing. On a practical level you are protecting your lover's precious skin: symbolically you are anointing him or her. The custom of bathing a revered or beloved object in oil is ancient and common to many religions. In oiling your lover you are honouring him or her with a sacred and traditional act.

Understanding Your Lover
When it comes to reading your lover with your hands the simplest rule is this: tense muscles tighten and as a result feel harder to the touch than relaxed ones. As you run your hands over your lover you will discover the patterns of the body below the surface, learning them with care and intimacy.

Rubbing on tight muscles produces very different sensations in different people, and the degree of pressure will need to vary likewise. What to one person is deeply pleasurable will be to another intolerably painful: another will feel 'grateful pain', where the sensation is sore but welcome as it begins to loosen the knotted muscle. If your lover begins to tense up you are pressing too hard: the whole idea is to relax, not tense. You will learn, too, to listen to his or her voice: a relaxed throat produces sighs, moans, clear notes of satisfaction, whilst a tense one produces whimpers and snarls. This is learning about your lover as a working body, a miracle of anatomy under your hands.

Each massage should begin and end with some open-palm rubbing, pushing any toxins squeezed from the muscles towards the cleansing lymph glands – which is to say to the upper shoulders from the back, to the armpits from the upper arms and inner elbows from the forearms, to the groin from the inner thighs and the backs of the knees from the calves. (These, be advised, are areas you should not massage too firmly – you do not want to damage the glands.) This stroke, known as 'effleurage' in Swedish massage, is the 'open and close' of your encounter, the greeting and farewell to your lover's body.

Caressing Touches

Beyond these strokes there is a courteous caress. Before you start and finish a massage rest both your hands flat against your partner. Feel the connection between the two of you: let your palms warm his or her skin. Remember, too, the simple rule: never let both of your hands leave your lover's body. Lying there uncertain where the next touch will fall is not as soothing as maintaining a constant physical connection: if you need to get up to change position or add more oil, remember to keep one hand lightly in contact.

Finally be respectful of your own body. Be careful of your back and ensure that your posture doesn't strain it. When leaning down hold your arms straight and let your weight rather than your arms do the work.

With the understanding of these basics massage becomes an open road.

Back Massage

The spine holds us upright and holds us together. In our backs we gather most of the tensions and burdens of life: from the back we walk, stand and make love. To honour your lover's back is to honour his or her centre.

Begin by laying your hands on your partner's hips. Smooth upwards from hips to shoulder, being careful of the unprotected kidneys. So soothing is this manoeuvre that you may carry on for a long, long moment without losing your partner's devotion.

Next interlace your fingers and rub in circles up along one side of the spine, then the other. The muscles that hold the spine upright lie along-side it like twin snakes: as you move them to and fro, your partner will feel the tension release. Next rub around the shoulder blades: knots often gather between the scapula and the spine and thrive on some attention. This strong, bony area may also enjoy 'hacking', rhythmically chopping with the sides of both hands, your wrists and fingers loose and floppy. Finally move your rubbing to the shoulder itself, kneading the strong muscles at the top.

When you are done ask your partner to turn over. Standing at his or her head run your hands along the shoulders and scoop up along the neck, pulling gently: this is a motion so comforting the recipient can feel as tended to as a child. Scoop again and again along the neck, letting your fingers work the muscles. After this cradle your lover's head in your hands and turn it on one side, holding it with your lower hand and massaging his or her scalp with your fingertips, then turn it the other way to finish. Scoop up the neck a final time and over the head, letting your fingers lift off the top of the scalp as if pulling all your partner's troubles out and away.

Hands and Feet

With our feet we walk, skip and run to our lovers: with our hands we caress, gesticulate and communicate. Our hands and feet dance us through the world: what we do with them makes us human. To honour our lover's hands and feet is to greet them.

Hands and feet are not unlike: both are evolved from the paws of our limber ancestors, and consequently massaging them is similar. Begin by smoothing oil over them, holding them tenderly between your palms. This gesture is particularly moving, making the recipient feel loved and appreciated.

Wrists and Ankles

Our hands and feet begin with the wrists and ankles. Start with a satisfying rub around those bones before moving on to the points where tension gathers; the insteps of the feet, the flesh between thumb and forefinger in the hands. Hold the hand or foot and bend it to and fro as if trying to make the sides fold together. This lets the bones move and loosen.

Rub firmly with your fingertips across the heels and balls of the feet. These are covered with a fine but sturdy layer of flesh and have strong bones underneath, so they can enjoy a good going over. The backs of the hands and tops of the feet are more thinly covered, so smooth over gently with your thumbs, stroking rather than pushing too much. Cover the whole area fully with your touch.

Move on to the fingers and toes. Rub each one individually up along the sides, swirling with your fingertips and pulling gently to let any tension release: when finished, grip each in your fist for a moment and slide off the top.

To conclude this massage hold each hand or foot firmly between your palms again for a long moment before laying them down somewhere comfortable and letting go.

Arms and Legs

With our arms we reach into the world:
with our legs we stride through it. To
massage our lover's limbs is to ease the
passage through life. The arms and legs
are similar in their nature to hands and
feet, and can be approached similarly.

Begin at the ankles or wrists and
stroke up the whole limb for a while
to warm it. After this start again at
the bottom. When massaging the leg
use a firm upwards stroke against the
calf from the heel to the knee (taking
care to avoid the delicate fold of the
knee itself). With the arm, hold the
hand in your own left hand and gently
pinch the forearm between the fingers
and thumb of your right, drawing
downwards to the elbow in a 'draining'
stroke. Move upwards to the thigh or
upper arm, rubbing and rolling the
large muscle under your hands to give
it a warm workout. Finally return to
caressing the whole limb again before
lifting right off at the shoulder or hip.

Genital Massage

The caressing of our lover's intimate parts is a foundation stone in a joyous relationship. To nurture someone's sexual organs is to embrace him or her as a sexual being, to nourish and welcome them with an open heart. On a practical level such massage is also an excellent way of exploring your partner's pleasure zones. There is nothing like sitting back and watching as your fingers do the walking to learn how best to satisfy your beloved.

Orgasm on Schedule?
There are few things worse for sex than a ticking clock. When we are passively accepting pleasure from a lover, there is a tendency to feel we must race towards orgasm as fast as possible to spare his or her efforts – rather a diffident way to receive anyone's generosity. It can often seem as if we have some kind of mental schedule in sex, in which any deviation from the plan counts as a failure. Sex turns into the sensual equivalent of an exam nightmare. The root of this nightmare is simple: we're prone to judge the quality of a sexual experience entirely by the orgasm. When you think about it this is a meagre standard. It's as if we go to a concert, listen to the orchestra play a beautiful symphony, then go home thinking of nothing except how they played the last twenty bars. If we knew a music lover who judged concerts this way, we'd consider them eccentric at best.

It helps to consider hand-to-genital caresses as a massage rather than as a 'hand job'. Orgasm may or may not result but this is not a proof that we've done things 'right'. Genital massage is not a test, but a sensual exchange. When we allow ourselves to be massaged without worrying about orgasm, we open ourselves up to an experience of pleasure that lets us enjoy every single moment.

For Him

For a man the experience of self-pleasuring tends to be a satisfying simple rub up and down his penis – a stroke as fine and basic as walking, but not the only delight his body is capable of yielding. Men are expected to focus their attention entirely on the penis, but this massage lets a man experience his genitals as a whole, widening his capacity for delight.

Complete Genital Massage

Massage around your lover's penis: for this exercise it is not important whether or not he is erect – your lover may find a profound relief if there are reduced expectations. Begin by stimulating around the base, down between the buttocks and around the testicles. Massage the testicles themselves gently, letting them roll backwards and forwards under your fingers, then move to the perineum – the area between the testicles and the anus. Rub this sensitive area with good firm pressure – within it is the sensitive prostate, seat of much bliss.

If your partner becomes erect, massage up and down the shaft a little bit but don't pay too much attention to the head or frenulum – the idea is to spin this massage out. If your partner finds himself growing frustrated, he should centre himself in a breathing meditation, letting the anticipation wash through him without reaching for a hasty conclusion.

Orgasm may result naturally, or you may eventually decide to move upwards and induce a climax, but the aim of this massage is to let both of you relax into discovering that a man does not need to come within a few seconds to be considered a man. Take time to enjoy the complex and beautiful configuration of organs that show your lover's masculinity, and let him relax into the diffuse pleasures.

Feather-Touch Penis Massage

Stimulate your partner gently until he's erect. With your one hand support the base of his penis: you don't need to grip it, just prop it up comfortably so that you have easy access to all sides.

Now begin stroking. Start by touching him gently at the base of the shaft with just the tips of your forefinger and middle finger. Very, very lightly, run your fingers up the underside until you reach the frenulum. When you get there brush quickly over it – don't linger there – and trace a circle around the back of the head and around to the frenulum again. From there return your stroke to your starting point. The pattern you're tracing is basically an upright line with a loop at the top.

The important thing in this exercise is to build up a rhythm and keep it constant. Instead of dwelling on the glans and the frenulum you're gently teasing them. The course of your fingers takes in all the most sensitive parts of the penis, but it doesn't overwork them. Instead it builds up an ebb and flow of expectation that can become almost hypnotic. Breaking the rhythm can break the focus, but if that happens just return to it and build up again. To begin with the sensations will be fairly mild, but with the gathering excitement a man can end up writhing with pleasure.

This massage lets the couple fall into an intense harmony, becoming totally absorbed in one another. For the man the experience can be almost trance-like: instead of rushing towards climax he is completely present in the moment. Pleasure builds to an exquisite plateau at once relaxed and intense, and minute after minute stretches out into one long, glorious instant.

Single-Spot Penis Massage

Take your lover's erect penis and hold it upright. With your left hand if you're right-handed or vice versa, encircle the base of it with your thumb and forefinger, as if you were making an 'okay' gesture. Hold it, not gripping tight enough to be uncomfortable but with a secure clasp. Then lay your other thumb gently on the frenulum, just under the head, and begin a slow, circular massaging movement.

Simple though this sounds, for a man accustomed to pleasuring himself with an up and down stroke, this massage can produce an extraordinary pleasure drawn from deep within his body, an experience that can be profoundly moving. Whilst you enjoy the subtlety of your small movements, holding yourself relaxed and poised, your lover lies back and learns that his capacity for pleasure is more than he was taught to expect was possible.

Have the Freedom to Experiment

The ways to massage a man's genitals are many and various: some may lead to orgasm, others need not. A man undergoing such massages may choose to practise a breathing meditation, calming himself to a state where he can enjoy the sensations not as a headlong rush to climax but as a balmy plateau. A lover performing these massages, freed from haste, can experiment with different pressures, tempos and strokes, curling and twisting his or her hands as well as gliding up and down, pleasuring the penis as part of the greater whole instead of as a separate organ to be caressed in isolation.

Don't Leave Out the Other Parts!

Because a man's penis is the centre of his pleasure, displaying his arousal and climax with easy-to-see signals, you can focus on it at the expense of his other sensitive areas. Men sometimes

consider themselves thick-skinned compared with women, possessed of only one erogenous zone. In fact men are possessed of skins capable of yielding great pleasure: the pleasures of the penis are simply so intense that the rest of the body can be forgotten.

Whilst the penis should never be ignored or denigrated, it remains a shame to ignore the male body as a whole. To broaden our attention is not to reject the penis but to bring in other pleasures to keep it company. When performing a genital massage on a man, then, it can sometimes be rewarding to massage the thighs, stomach and chest, spreading out the caresses to let the man experience his body as a whole. When there is no hurry to reach orgasm there is no need to let the great capacity for pleasure the penis contains make us inattentive of the greater self.

Performing genital massage on a man, then, is a wonderful way to embrace his masculinity, honouring the penis not as a single organ but as a vital part of his entire, precious body.

For Her

Unlike men, women are not taught to see their genitals as a proud display. The female genitals, far from being seen as 'feminine', are often cast as dirty, an area to deodorize, douche, wax, shave and generally minimize. A boy may rejoice at the growth of his penis from childhood smallness to adult heft, but for a girl the 'perfect' organ is hairless, scentless, with small inner labia tucked invisibly within the outer lips – as it was when she was a child. A mature vulva is seen in much of popular culture as somehow disgusting.

This tragic misconception can make it very difficult for a woman to enjoy her lover's caresses – for what considerate person can truly enjoy someone's gift if she believes it a sacrifice?

A complete genital massage is a lovely way for a woman to experience herself as the beautiful adult she is.

Let the woman relax on a bed, her legs spread at a comfortable angle and propped on pillows if necessary. Have a ritual bath in which you focus your attention on honouring the woman – the cleaner she feels, the easier it will be for her to enjoy herself. Light candles, put on music and make the atmosphere as tranquil as possible.

Complete Genital Massage

Now begin the massage. A silicone-based lubricant is best because oil can block pores: smooth it gently over the whole area. Work from the outside in, beginning with her outer labia, her perineum and the sensitive skin between her buttocks. Move inwards, gently caressing, pulling and massaging the inner labia. Finally slide your fingers inside her, massaging all around and seeking the best spots whilst your other hand caresses her clitoris. As you massage her, picture the image of a flower, and visualize moving slowly from its petals towards its fragrant centre.

With this massage a lover learns where to touch his beloved, and the woman learns she can be open, exposed and treasured.

Plucking Massage

With your lover in a comfortable position smooth some lubricant around her labia, massaging her whole genital area lightly until she is pleasantly aroused but tranquil.

Run the tip of your thumb and forefinger up from below her vagina towards her clitoris, holding her inner lips in a delicate pinching gesture. When you reach her clitoris press your fingertips together so you take hold of it, and then pull off at the top as if plucking a string.

This is a massage that lets the woman experience pleasure in her clitoris as a rising and falling sensation. Instead of having to focus on coming as quickly as she can for fear her lover will be bored, the woman can relax, leaning back and breathing naturally, enjoying the moment with no need to stare anxiously at the clock.

Internal Massage

The inside of the vagina is a mysterious area to many. The penis may stimulate it during intercourse, but greater knowledge and understanding can be sought out and found with the sensitive, flexible fingers.

Using some lubricant begin by massaging gently around the opening of the vagina. Tantalize your lover, letting her enjoy the sensation with no need to hurry. When you are ready start slipping your massage a little deeper in. Begin with one finger (making sure the nail is short and smooth) and rub all the way around.

If you want to find the G-spot, turn your palm upwards and crook your finger as if beckoning: rub along the front wall and let your lover tell you how it feels. As she becomes relaxed you may choose to introduce more fingers. Explore all the way inside, from the entrance to the cervix, discovering your beloved's intimate structures. In this way a woman and man can learn together her deepest secrets.

Honouring Female Genitals

For a woman such massages are an act of acceptance like no other. For many women their own genitals can be something of a mystery: hidden from the eye, unpredictable in their reactions and something that 'good girls' don't take too unseemly an interest in. Where the female skin is generally smooth and sleek, the female genitals are frilled, colourful, exuberant so different in appearance from the

rest of her body that a woman insecure about her femininity can feel that her genitals are not a flower of her sexual self but some kind of aberration. In many cases the only person with real knowledge of her genitals is a nurse taking a swab: hardly a foundation for self-love or romance. When it comes to pleasure some sensations depend on stimulation in places a woman can't comfortably reach herself: many women depend on feeling assured that their genitals are not the ugly mess culture teaches them to believe they are, but a fine edifice, at once sturdy and subtle, which any true lover should consider himself privileged to touch.

To massage a woman's genitals is to honour a woman's beauty, not as a commercial product or a creation of make-up and presentation, but as a healthy, graceful creature, perfectly created for enjoyment and beautiful in her pleasure.

Conclusion

The gift of massage lets a couple go beyond the surface and know each other as they know no other bodies. Each assumes the role of healer and healed, teacher and student, fulfilling needs that go beyond the sexual into the physical and emotional, which serve to deepen the sexual connection.

Honouring Your Lover

At the root of a successful relationship is a deep love, not only for the beloved as a person but also a love for his or her well-being. A truly romantic lover strives for the highest of goals: for his or her lover to thrive and flourish, and through being there to make his or her lover's life a better place.

Massage is an essential and gratifying path to this happy outcome. We enjoy the pleasure of handling our partner's gorgeous flesh along with the pleasure of letting our partner's hands loosen our knots, probe our tensions and draw out

our sensuality. In rubbing each other's bodies we care for each other's hearts. Rather than seeing massage as foreplay or a non-sexual activity, we appreciate it best when we understand that in massage we seek to satisfy the beloved's body and honour his or her humanity, to show our love for his or her body with the skill and devotion of our own.

Both as a symbolic gesture in love-making rituals and as a simple means of soothing and stimulating our lovers, massage is an indispensable source of comfort and delight.

What Is Love-making?

Buried somewhere in most of us is the traditional answer: penetrative sexual intercourse between a man and a woman, which ends when the man climaxes. We know we've sometimes had more fun from other kinds of encounters, that putting too much expectation on a single act can end up with the man feeling pressurized and the woman feeling unsatisfied, and that same-sex couples make love just as joyfully with no such privileging of one gender's pleasure over another. However, when we hear the word 'sex', this is the act that most of us envision. As long as we ignore our bodies and bend our minds to this expectation we are short-changing ourselves.

6. *Taking it Slowly*

Broadening the Definition

It is wiser to redefine the concept in a way that speaks to our responsive flesh instead of to our categorizing minds. Why disparage acts just as delicious as penetrative sex by not considering them 'real' sex? Instead let us consider love-making as any act in a sexual relationship in which one person gives pleasure to the other. This is not to disparage penetrative sex. Like many other forms of love-making, it has pleasures all its own. By broadening our definition of love-making we do not reduce the importance of penetrative sex. We simply see the importance of all the other ways we can pleasure each other. These ways are not in competition with each other. All are in mutual harmony, pursuing the simple goal of helping ourselves and our lovers towards physical rejoicing.

Sex Versus Foreplay

It is most effective to consider any sensual encounter with your lover to have been an act of love-making. To do so immediately reduces a great deal of the pressure. For an encounter to have to be 'real' sex not only fosters resentment and self-condemnation, it is based on a false understanding of what is real. In fact you decide what is love-making in your relationship, and you decide what is real. Satisfying yourself and your partner matters far more than defining it.

Rather than following a pattern according to what 'counts', you can make love as you please, climaxing or not, stopping when you choose. The goal is not to have an orgasm: orgasm is lovely, but it is not the sole purpose. The purpose is physical pleasure – and if we believe that orgasm is the only physical pleasure we can experience, we have not been paying attention.

Yet Foreplay Is Sex

Similarly it is most effective to dismiss the notion of 'foreplay' from our minds. The very syllable 'fore' demotes the action of kissing, caressing, rubbing and delighting your partner into a mere preamble, the part that comes before the real business of the evening. Yet if we cannot be fully absorbed in kissing our lover's neck, we cannot be absorbed in any kind of love-making.

Worse the concept of foreplay tends to devalue the experiences of women. Because it generally takes longer for a woman to climax and she is less likely to come through penetrative sex, many of the things that most thrill and gratify the female partner are, by this word 'foreplay', reduced to a precursor, even to a job her partner has to perform if he wants any 'real' sex.

For our purposes we may go by a simple understanding – anything that pleases our partner is mindful sex.

Positions

What Positions Are Best?

When it comes to mindful sex the answer is a simple one: ask your body and listen to what it tells you. Rather than assume that one single, magical position will always be absolutely right, it is wise to bear in mind that different positions will please us most on different days, with different partners and different moods.

What are the positions to choose from? You will find a different answer from every source you ask. The *Kamasutra* for instance lists dozens: the sex researcher Albert Kinsey declared that there were basically six – man-on-top, woman-on-top, side-by-side, man-behind-woman, sitting and standing – which couples could vary according to their own desires. For the sake of ease, we will use these basic classifications, always remembering that couples can adjust and adapt the positions to suit their own desires.

Missionary Position

The man-on-top, or 'missionary', position is traditional in much of Western culture. The woman may lay her legs along the bed to narrow and flatten her vagina, plant her feet, wrap her legs around her lover's hips or raise them high in the air to enable deeper penetration. When it comes to mindful sex the advantages of this position are that it brings the lovers face to face. To increase the mindfulness of this position breathing together and prolonged eye contact can be practised: it is highly sociable.

Woman On Top

The woman-on-top position is likewise very companionable. The woman may, if she chooses, face away from her lover so he views her back, in which case the position becomes closer to rear entry, only with the woman in full control of the motion: most couples, however, prefer to make love in this position face to face. As with the missionary position the couple can maintain eye contact: this is also a position that gives couples a fuller vision of each other's bodies. As the woman dances on top of her lover she can also delight in her view of him.

A variant of man-on-top love-making lets the man sit back between his lover's legs, penetrating the woman as she reclines. In terms of position and vision this is close to a male equivalent of the woman-on-top experience: dancing over a partner who lies naked and lovely before you. In practical terms this position allows for deep penetration, man and woman seeking to bury themselves in each other.

In both positions where one partner lies on their back there is the chance to experience receptivity versus activity. The reclining partner may relax, giving him- or herself up to a meditative experience of sensation temporarily, whilst the partner on top experiences meditation in action, knowing his or her body through motion. This is not to say that the reclining partner need not move: indeed a co-operative motion is often helpful, but the differences allow for a variety of emotional states that the couple will thrive on exploring.

Side-by-side Love-making

This position allows for a mutuality: the couple may already see themselves as equals, but side-by-side involves a parity of position and motion that lets them enact this equality with their bodies as well as their souls. To make love side-by-side the couple needs to be sure their position is comfortable for both. The woman's lower leg may go to sleep if the man lies on it too long or at the wrong angle. This is a position in which the couple may experience their bodies moving together in a search for shared comfort that shows tenderness.

Sitting and Standing

The mutuality is also true of sitting love-making, with the additional effect that to sit up is to be alert, wakeful in the world. This is even more so when standing and love-making. Rather than lying down and assuming a position of rest, the lovers remain in the same stances they would assume to face the day: head up, face forwards. To make love in these positions is to know that we are always in the world, always sexual and that intercourse is one amongst many steps in the dance.

Rear Entry Position

The last of the basic positions is known as rear entry, vulgarly referred to as 'doggy' style, a slang term that leads many women to fear it is degrading. There is indeed a striking effect in being unable to see your partner's face, but it need not be a depersonalizing one. In rear entry positions the man becomes all but invisible to the woman, and from the man's view the woman becomes a body, a graceful form in a position that accentuates the feminine hourglass shape. Because of this, rear entry is a position in which the lovers may experience each other, not as objects to degrade but as incarnations of universal principle – one person as the perfect, fleshly embodiment of femininity, or masculinity. To know each other as Man and Woman as well as knowing each other as John and Jane is no degradation, but an honouring of the other's most fundamental, simplest self.

Using Your Imagination

These are the basic positions of love-making. If it pleases you to study them in more detail, the *Kama-sutra* and many other books discuss the variations and subtleties a couple may experiment with. For yourself,

however, you may well find that the best way to discover a new position is in bed rather than in a book. Wind around your lover's limbs and discover what pleasures are in store. In terms of mindfulness the principle is straightforward: Love-making is not a mechanical act but a physical conversation, a way of allowing one body to communicate with another. Choosing a position is choosing the tone of that conversation.

Some couples may find that some positions never suit them, others may like to try as wide a variety as possible to keep things lively. As long as we never fall into a routine of doing the same thing absentmindedly time after time there is no right or wrong way. There is only the way you and your lover find for yourselves with a mindful appreciation of your own sensations and our own emotions as your guide.

Fitting Together

When experimenting with positions the most important thing to remember is fit. Men are well aware that they vary in penis size – both length and girth – but women vary as well. Natural configuration and childbearing for instance can affect the width of a woman's vagina: meanwhile some penises show their erection in short, full expansion, whilst others grow long and narrow. With a wide-set vagina and a narrow penis for instance stimulation may not be all the couple wants, and positions where the woman is able to press her legs together such as rising on her hands and knees will suit such a couple better.

Equally important is the position of a woman's cervix (the neck of her womb). In some women this sits deep inside, but in others it naturally rides only five to eight centimetres (two or three inches) above the entrance, and many women find it painful to have it

knocked – probably the closest a woman comes to the experience of a blow to the testicles. With arousal it tends to lift higher up, but a couple who combine a low cervix and a long penis will do well to avoid the deeper-penetrating positions, or to perform them with care and gentleness if the woman is to have a pleasurable time.

Angles and Tilts

Also to be remembered is angle. Although heterosexual men do not usually see other men's erect penises, there is a surprising variety of positions they can assume. Some penises point straight forwards; others rise on an upwards incline; others grow stiff but angle downwards; some lean to the left or the right. Some erections are straight as arrows; some curve or bend upwards, downwards or sideways. There is no 'good' or 'bad' shape for an erection: a man who honours his body will know that the shape his erect penis assumes is simply the natural shape that is right for him, and any woman who honours her lover will know that however it looks, his erection is beautiful.

Women meanwhile have vaginas that also tilt or angle this way and that, and which contain different pleasure spots. The famous G-spot for instance is located at the front of the vagina two or three centimetres (an inch or so) in, and the lesser-known A-spot is supposedly located higher up, just under the cervix – debates rage about exactly where, but a thoughtful exploration with a lover's finger is by far the best answer to the question. For some women internal stimulation is a gateway to paradise: for others external pleasuring of the clitoris is the finest of sensations. Mindful trial and error is by far the most reliable source of information: if your body contradicts a book, always listen to your body.

Each Fit Is Individual

As a couple becomes familiar with one another they will learn which positions work well for them and which do not. A couple where the man's erection angles upwards and the woman's vagina angles towards the front of her body may find it difficult to make love with the woman on top and facing the man's feet: such a position bends the penis downwards in a way that could hurt this particular man. On the other hand if the woman sits astride her lover facing his head and leans forwards, the fit will be comfortable for both.

Combining your bodies in different positions is more than just looking at a diagram. The subtleties of an individual body are beyond anyone generalizing to guess at. The main thing to remember is that your anatomy is perfectly your own and beautiful in its uniqueness. Work with what you have and it will reward you for your attention.

Rhythm

We humans are creatures of rhythm. Before we are born into the world we are held contained within our mothers' wombs, lulled by the sound of a heart-beat: at the moment of birth we draw the first of a great chain of breaths that will be the rhythm of our lives. Day by day we follow the rhythm of sunset and sunrise: year by year summer follows spring as Earth leans towards the sun and spins away again. Walking, chewing, talking, we pace out our lives to the rhythm of our own bodies.

To enjoy rhythm in sex is to rejoice in our essential natures as dancers to the beat of life. We can let it absorb us utterly, feeling ourselves as rocked by rhythm as the sands on the shore.

Varying the Tempo

When we understand our bodies' grace we understand that the movement of our hips in love-making is more than just a pragmatic gesture to generate friction. With rhythm we can tease or delight or overwhelm our lover, suiting our tempo to our moods as we would dance different steps to different music.

Variation adds to the pleasure of movement. Whilst sometimes we may most enjoy an energetic up-and-down motion we can also vary the speed of our strokes, alternating short, short, long, short, short, long, drawing out our satisfaction with ever-increasing depth or force. Try alternating gentle and hard strokes, shallow and deep, not at random but in regular patterns, generating melody with your own body.

Rhythm is life, yet it is also fun. Why else would people dance and stamp when they are happy? When we are filled with joy it is in our nature to move in time. As you make love with your partner let joy strum through you, and let the motion of your body be your dance, your physical expression of the happiness within.

Making Love With Our Mouths

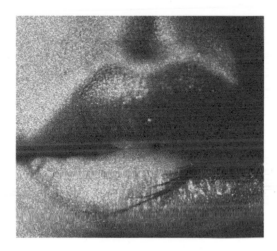

Our lips and tongues are amongst the great givers and receivers of joy: the cool flow of water or the warm taste of food, the thrill of a kiss, the fascination of speech. When we turn our mouths to pleasuring our lovers' most intimate organs we are using our most mobile of instruments: we kiss, we speak and we go down with our mouths.

Complete Dedication

To let a lover pleasure us orally is one of the most meditative of the sexual experiences: totally attended to by our generous partner we are able to relax and let the sensations absorb us utterly. To go down on a partner is one of the deepest and finest ways of honouring their bodies. In touch and taste we receive and coax them into delight, dedicating ourselves completely to the experience of gratifying another human being.

In Tantric terminology oral sex is enchantingly known as 'playing the flute' (when done for a man) and 'polishing the pearl' (when done for a woman, although scientific knowledge has since identified the clitoris not as a small pearl but as a large organ mostly buried inside the body with tendrils in several directions: it is more like a small octopus than a pearl in fact.) Our own terminology may not be so poetic, but the phrase 'oral sex' does at least acknowledge that oral sex is sex, an act of love-making rather than a precursor to it.

Female Pleasure

Oral sex is in fact essential to most happy relationships. For a woman who does not climax through penetrative sex – or even a woman who does – her lover's tongue is as beloved to her and as vital a part of his love and virility as his penis. Far from being the second-best option, pleasuring a woman with your tongue is one of the most powerful ways to impress upon her your expertise, your skill and stamina – your manhood.

Women are educated to believe they should be pleasing to men: Freud and his followers had the confused idea that for a woman to enjoy clitoral stimulation more than penetration was a sign of 'immaturity'. This notion is now generally understood as silly, in fact hostile to women's true nature, but it can be hard for a woman to let go of the idea that she should be working to make her man feel good.

Accepting the gift of oral stimulation from him, she learns with her body that her pleasure is valid, essential and to be rejoiced in. A man whose mouth can please a woman will find her entirely willing to honour him.

When pleasuring a woman for instance the variety of caresses is wide. Lick against her clitoris with your tongue soft and relaxed: strike against it with your tongue rigid. Graze the tip of your tongue against her labia, tantalizing her with sensation. Suck the whole of her clitoris into your mouth, letting the sensation pull the pleasure out of her. Lick at the opening of her vagina, tasting her deep inside. When a woman is entranced she often freezes: when you have found the rhythm that works do not speed up but carry on exactly as before, listening as her excitement swells and she becomes overwhelmed with joy.

143

And for Men ...

Oral sex is so precious to men that it's practically proverbial, the subject of many jokes. Yet it is a serious matter as well. Whilst massage and exploration may open up new channels of pleasure to a man his penis will almost always remain the locus of his pleasure and his sense of manhood. Men are often told that a gentleman does not press his sexual demands on a lady: teenage boys struggle to hide their embarrassing erections; men tease and compete over penis size; women who are tired of the 'machismo' make jokes about penis obsession that may inadvertently discourage a gentler man.

A man with a considerate heart in fact spends much of his time hearing one way or another that his penis is not welcome. The experience of a woman's soft lips and warm tongue licking and enwrapping it lets a man know that with this beloved woman, his penis is more than welcome: it is beautiful, delectable, embraced. Such a woman is in turn beautiful, delectable and embraced in the vision of her lover.

As with women there is more than one way to pleasure a man. The traditional sucking gesture, where the woman shields her teeth with her lips and takes her lover's penis fully into her mouth, moving up and down on the shaft, is most effective, especially when she flicks her tongue against the sensitive underside of the penis as she glides, but there are other delights too. Flick your tongue up and down the underside, teasing the sensitive skin: suck at the frenulum like a sweet. Bring your hands into play, holding the penis below where your mouth encloses it, turning and twisting as you ride up and down. Try a variant of the feather-touch massage using the tip of your tongue instead of your fingers. There is a world of possibility.

Express and Explore

Whether performed one at a time or in the mutual 'sixty-nine' position, oral love-making is a matter of exploration and discovery. Different lovers enjoy different sensations and this is the time to try. As with mouth-to-mouth kissing, to caress with the mouth is not just a means of evoking sensation – a kiss is the great expression of love. When we feel passion or tenderness, when we yearn to show respect and honour a person, our instinct is to touch our mouths against them. There are as many kisses and expressions of our tongues and lips as there are words. When we make love with our mouths, we kiss our partner's sexual centre: we thrill them and shower them with emotional devotion.

Anal Sex

For many people anal penetration is one of the last taboos. For others, however, anal stimulation is one of the most delectable acts possible.

Different anatomies respond differently. There are a great many nerve endings around the anal passage, and in both sexes these can respond with great enthusiasm to the right kind of touch. For women anal penetration can also press against the sensitive spots in the vagina such as the G-spot: for men it can stimulate the prostate, sometimes allowing for an 'internal' experience of orgasm.

Overcoming Judgements

A man who likes to be stimulated anally is not unmanly: stimulation of the prostate is after all stimulation of a uniquely male organ. To believe that it weakens a man is to believe that there is something lesser about being the penetrated lover – an attitude that

hardly squares with respect for women. Likewise a woman who likes anal stimulation is not a cheap or degraded person, merely a woman who knows how to listen to her own body and has sufficient self esteem not to let the judgement of others shame her out of her own pleasures. Anal pleasure is one of those things people either like or they don't – your own body is your best guide.

Hygiene is an unusually important consideration when it comes to anal sex, and managing this without feeling too clinical can be a challenge. The anal passage contains a great number of bacteria that, whilst fine in their place, are best kept there. Penetration with naked fingers therefore is not recommended because microbes can easily get trapped under the nails: similarly it is wise to use a condom to cover the penis or any sex toy, and you should never move from penetrating the anus to penetrating the vagina without a change of protection.

Being Mindful Throughout

Mindfulness can help in two ways here. The first is helping us to accept our bodies without squeamishness: when we are fully present in our bodies we understand that to take precautions is not to insult ourselves, but merely to recognise the reality that some microbes should stay where they are. The second is in helping us see that, as with any kind of safety measure, it need not interrupt the moment unless we divide the world into sexual and non-sexual, part of the act and alien to the act. Donning a condom or pair of surgical gloves can be as ceremonial as oiling a lover or preparing a bed if we are tranquil enough in ourselves to see it.

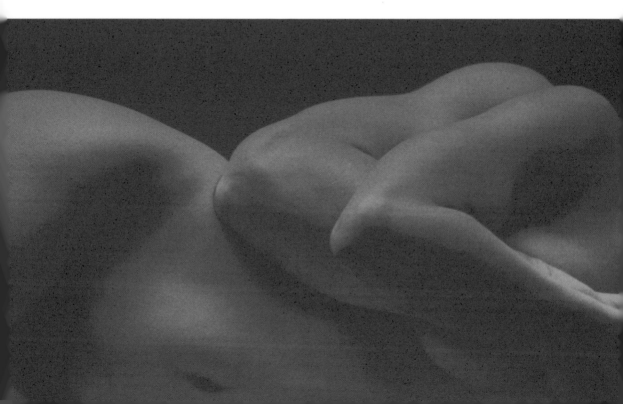

Lubrication

The other practicality to remember is lubricant. Unlike the vagina, which is self-cleaning and naturally moist, the anal passage is designed to absorb moisture: penetrating it without lubrication can be painful and even cause injuries. Oil-based lubricants will eat your protective rubber, so a water- or silicone-based product is your friend, preferably a fairly thick one for maximum moisture: sex shops and websites sell a good variety.

All this can feel a bit technical if we are already nervous. To address this it may be useful to practise a pre-love-making ritual in which the condom or gloves and lubricants are laid on your altar with the foodstuffs and candles. Treating them as ritual objects recognises their significance: to let you satisfy your lover's body whilst treasuring his or her health and well-being. In this way we show ourselves that safeguards and aids are no less sacred than the candles we light: they, too, are simply objects that help us enrich our sex lives.

Relax Into It

When it comes to anal penetration gentleness and slowness are the best way. Begin by massaging the area around the opening with plenty of lubricant: this in itself is a wonderful sensation and may well be enough to satisfy those who do not enjoy penetration itself. When your lover is fully relaxed you may begin penetration. Generally the muscles contract – rather than fighting against them, pause, allow them to accustom themselves to the sensation, then proceed a little further. As you become more experienced with your lover's responses you may move more confidently, but always begin carefully. With such delicate skin it is better

to be too gentle than too rough. Whilst not to everybody's taste, anal penetration can, in its very taboo quality, melt away a barrier to trust and increase our mindfulness. Making love in ways we have been taught to shun can bind us together, showing that we judge only by each other's pleasure and not by the strictures of the world. With such enjoyment we can relax into the knowledge that our partner truly loves and knows us completely.

Taking a Walk On the Wild Side

Some people like to spice their love-making up with fantasy, playing roles, toying with symbolic power exchanges and trying out a wider variety of sensations, including pain. If your imagination runs that way, is it possible to balance this with mindfulness and ethics? In fact there is no reason to exclude such treats if that's the way your dreams incline: you just need to be sure you know what you're about.

Why Do We Categorize?

Western traditions tend to separate and categorize sexuality, but it's good to remember that our categories are not absolute. The distinctions of 'homosexual', 'heterosexual' and 'bisexual' would for instance have meant very little to an ancient Greek living in a culture where who you slept with and which gender they were was no particular marker of your identity. Similarly there are some activities

that Westerners class as 'fetish' that are considered in some Eastern traditions to be merely part of the repertoire of love-making. The *Kama-sutra* for instance not only discusses different methods of striking, scratching and biting your lover, but pays respectful attention to the different kinds of marks you may choose to create.

If you feel inclined to try some experimentation, there is no need to let the fear of being some kind of pervert stop you. Your erotic imagination is precious and its promptings are always worth listening to.

Compatible Fantasies

You must of course be tender of your lover's feelings. There is no excuse for pressuring a partner into an act he or she finds distasteful. Experimentation by mutual consent is one thing and it is great to try new ideas and explore whether or not they please you: it is even worth trying something again after an unsuccessful first attempt if it is important to your imagination. The first time we try anything our lack of skill may hinder us.

But whilst sometimes we hold back from trying a new thing because we fear being thought dirty or weird, sometimes we simply don't want to do it – *cannot* want to do it because it is alien to our sexual selves. Whilst some people enjoy a variety of roles, a man who dreams solely of serving a goddess may feel wrong playing a harsh lord, whilst a woman who yearns for innocence may likewise feel wrong playing the capricious goddess. To force or manipulate either into a role so alien to their sexual natures is nothing less than a violation, not because they are judgemental or prudish but because they have been made to hide their true sexual self, the self that yearns for recognition and which deserves to be honoured. Compatibility therefore is of the essence when playing more extreme games, and a loving couple will understand that it is as important to be honest as it is to be kind when discussing such a vulnerable subject.

Staying Safe

In the event that you and your partner find there is a wilder fantasy you both would like to explore, you should remember that your first and last commitment is that you must never, ever harm your partner. When playing riskier games it is wise to inform yourself as much as possible. There are excellent books on the subject, and most towns contain a friendly sado-masochistic community who are happy to give advice.

The techniques of safe play are too complex to pay full attention to here, but we can consider a few basics to begin with.

Consent is absolute and must always be observed. The common method used in the West is to have a 'safe word' that either partner can say if they want to call a halt: this lets them play whilst saying such words as 'No!' and 'Help!' without ending the love-making. The safe word is often a word one would not usually say such as 'guava': many people also choose to say 'red' for 'Stop',' 'yellow' for 'Slow down' and sometimes 'green' for 'Please do that more', but you can choose your own. Once a safe word is spoken, everything stops at once and both partners step out of their roles.

Start Slowly

For most people pain is felt as pleasure in the same way that a little spice adds to the deliciousness of a meal. Just as one wouldn't bite straight into a chilli, most people don't derive pleasure from pain without some warming up. If one is slapping, scratching or nibbling one's beloved, it is a good idea to begin gently and gradually increase the pressure, interspersing it with sensuous caresses to keep them aroused.

This allows the body to release endorphins, the same chemicals that create a 'runner's high' and that let the body process the sensations in a different and more erotic way than it would if it were struck cold. Be sure you understand enough basic anatomy to know what is safe. Strike only areas well padded with muscle and fat such as the buttocks, thighs, back and calves (and breasts if you are careful): avoid delicate bones and unprotected organs such as intestines and kidneys.

Understand What You're Doing

Most injuries in erotic games arise from careless binding. If you want to play in this way, again be sure you understand anatomy. Be especially careful of the lymph glands where they lie near the skin: at the backs of the knees, inside the elbows and under the arms and collarbone. Do not tie anything tight enough to cut off circulation – and be aware that stretchy bindings may tighten unexpectedly, so choose something reliable. Never tie anything around the neck, even loosely: accidents happen, and accidents that impede breathing can be fatal. Always keep to hand a pair of scissors so you can cut your beloved loose immediately if a crisis occurs, and never leave a bound lover alone, not even for a minute.

There is no reason to feel ashamed of your erotic imagination as long as you are ethical in exploring it. Risky games call for a degree of expertise, and expertise is of the conscious mind. We can be completely, meditatively present if we have carefully practised all the difficult things prior to love-making: this way we will not be distracted from ourselves by a tricky knot or be shaken from our entrancement by worrying that our lover does not know what he or she is doing. Our repertoire can be as narrow or as broad as we choose to make it, as long as we honour the rights of each other and ourselves and are committed to ensuring we know enough not to violate them accidentally.

Mindfulness and Role-Play

Is it unmindful to act a role rather than to make love as yourself? Not necessarily. The important thing is to understand which element of yourself the role expresses: enacting a certain side of yourself can indeed focus your mind. We can be present in our own flesh no matter what name we call ourselves. Role-play can simply be another form of ritual. We should never mistake the role for the whole of ourselves, but neither need we reject the part of ourselves the role calls forth.

Conclusion

There are so many ways of love-making, we can spend a lifetime exploring them. When it comes to mindfulness there is no right and wrong way: only ways that delight us and our partner mutually.

Ethics, Mindfulness and Love-making
Some philosophies see sexual union as an act that symbolically unites the masculine and feminine principles as a route to higher consciousness. Tantra is the path to explore if the spiritual side appeals to you: however, it is quite possible to enrich our lives, body and soul, with a simple, mindful approach to love-making. Human beings who seek ethics and insight in all paths of their lives are living a spiritually wholesome existence whether they adhere to a philosophy or not. With sex being an area where we often act out our confusions and shortcomings, a healthy and joyful attitude is the foundation of a truly good life.

When we are mindful, love-making cannot become routine: every moment is new. When we are mindful we are sensitive lovers: we honour our partner's feelings no more or less than our own. We recognise that an honest understanding of our own pleasure is a compliment to a loving dedication to our partner's. To be aware of the infinite variety that surrounds us is to at once steady and energize ourselves. And when we have this resource we are ready to make love.

The erotic connection we can make with another will change from partner to partner and moment to moment. Rather than chasing some idea of perfection or struggling to replicate an idealized past, with mindfulness we learn that there are a multitude of paths to joy. However, our bodies are intertwined with our lover's, there is beauty in every moment. We need only open our eyes.

Afterword

As we deepen our understanding of ourselves, our sexuality – which is so vital an element of our essential nature – comes to flower. Love-making, either with ourselves or with another, is how we remind our bodies that whatever the difficulties of the world we were not born to seek suffering but joy.

Reminding Us Who We Are

The emotions of love-making, whether in accepting ourselves or in loving another person, can be passionate, wild and extreme. This is all part of the ride, the glorious flurry of feeling that our restless hearts long for: the rush of experience that lets us know we are truly alive. Yet the dazzling power of that ride can leave us breathless and lost, unsure of ourselves. Its charm and glamour can leave us wondering whether our plain old selves are really exciting enough to merit such drama. To enjoy the ride we need a rich and steady centre, a strong conviction that this is who we truly are and that who we are is truly, bountifully enough.

Be Joyful in the Present

For this we need mindfulness. When we are present in the moment we enjoy every second that passes – and with that enjoyment grows assurance, a rich knowledge of the plenty that the world holds, the plenty within us and our great capacity to play between the two. A soul that can sit with itself and feel the world as it is is a soul ready for joy.

And it is joy that allows us finally to be steady. Not as sacrifice or asceticism, not as self-suppression, but as human beings confident that happiness is within our reach. Our capacity for pleasure traces across our skins in thousands and millions of nerve endings: our capacity for peace lies ready within our hearts whenever we choose to find it.

It is this, the play between tranquillity and passion, which lets us rejoice in ourselves: our ordinary, unique, astonishing selves. Love-making shakes us to our core: mindfulness holds that core unshakable.

Index

Footnotes

1. *The European Men's Condom Study*, Center for Sexual Health Promotion, Indiana University, Bloomington, website: www.condomerie.com/fitfeel/

2. *"Just smile, you'll feel better!" Will you? Really?"* Cognitive Daily Psychology Science Blog website: http://tiny.cc/qJ2cG

3. *The Miracle of Mindfulness*, Thich Nhat Hanh, published by Rider, an imprint of Random House, 1991

4 *'Le mieux est l'ennemi du bien', La Béguele, Conte Moral*, Voltaire, 1772

5. *Ways of Seeing*, John Berger, published by the BBC and Penguin, 1972

6 *Living with Depression*, UK National Health Service website: www.nhs.uk/Livewell/Depression/Pages/Depressionhome.aspx

7. Society for Sacred Sexuality website: www.sss-now.org/sacred_sex/archive/tantras.htm

8 *Les Misérables*, Victor Hugo, published by Penguin, 1976